# Trailside's Trail Food

By the Editors of

Magazine

## Edited by John Viehman
Host of "Trailside: Make Your Own Adventure"
and Executive Editor of BACKPACKER Magazine

Rodale Press, Emmaus, Pennsylvania

OUR MISSION

*We publish books that empower people's lives.*

RODALE BOOKS

Compiled by Laurence Wiland
Editor: John Viehman
Managing editor: Tom Shealey

Cover designer: Stan Green
Interior designer: John Pepper
Copy editor: Nancy Humes
Cover photographer: Mitch Mandel

If you have any questions or comments regarding this book, please write:
Rodale Press
Book Readers' Service
33 East Minor Street
Emmaus, PA 18098

ISBN 0-87596-169-X paperback

**Distributed in the book trade by St. Martin's Press**

2  4  6  8  10  9  7  5  3          paperback

# CONTENTS

# INTRODUCTION

On the trail, your body is the vehicle that transports your backpack, and like any machine, it needs fuel to create the power necessary to make it perform well. Food is your fuel. It's a pretty simple concept until you consider that healthy, high-performance food must meet some pretty stiff criteria. It should:

1) contain caloric and nutritive value
2) weigh next to nothing
3) taste good
4) cook up fast with minimal equipment
5) withstand temperature extremes, rough handling, and spoilage
6) be compact
7) cost little (if you're like most of us)

Obviously, there's more to trail food than meets the eye. What you choose to carry in your pack is only half the equation; you must also carry information in your head about food preparation, nutrition, and safety. This book will help you figure out what your body needs to stay healthy on the trail and offers a few pointers about culinary equipment and preparation.

There are also easy-to-prepare, trail-tested recipes demonstrated on "Trailside: Make Your Own Adventure" on PBS. Whether you're cooking for two in the snows of Montana or making a single-serving meal on the beaches of Baja, *Trailside's Trail Food* will make your adventure even more palatable.

See you on "Trailside."

**John Viehman**
Host, "Trailside: Make Your Own Adventure"
and Executive Editor, *Backpacker* Magazine

*chapter one:*
# WHAT A BACKPACKING BODY NEEDS

## Why Do I Get Exhausted On The Trail?

It has probably happened to you. You've hiked all day, and as the sun is slipping behind the ridge, you realize you've pushed too hard—should have paced yourself better. You've stopped looking for a prime campsite, because at this point, any old spot will do; all you want out of life is to drop the @#$%! pack that gains a ton with each step. Activity failure because of energy failure has probably ruined more backpacking trips than rain.

Terrain, your level of fitness, and weather all contribute to exhaustion, but the biggest, easiest-to-prevent problem comes when you don't get enough energy from food and fluids. Your digestive system breaks everything you eat into glucose, which is stored in muscle cells as glycogen and flows through your body in your blood. Ultimately, it's converted into energy. What you eat—your choice of fuel, so to speak—affects how well this all works and the amount of energy released.

For maximum performance on the trail, your diet should be about 70 percent carbohydrates, 15 percent protein, and 15 percent fat. Here's why:

**Carbohydrates**, commonly known as sugars and starches, rapidly break down into glucose during digestion and are stored for quick energy. Your storage capacity is small, though, so during a strenuous activity like backpacking, blood sugar levels can drop dramatically in a single hour. To keep your blood sugar and energy levels high, you need a regular intake of complex carbohydrates, such as fresh or dried fruits, low-fat cookies, bagels, muffins, rice cakes, and energy bars. In other words, snack like crazy!

Consuming a high-carbohydrate diet (70 to 80 percent carbos) for several days before a trip will double your glycogen stores and increase your on-trail performance as much as three times. Foods rich in carbohydrates include whole-grain breads and rolls, beans and peas, bulghur, lentils, oatmeal, pasta, brown rice, cereals, fruits, vegetables, applesauce, juices, and potatoes.

**Proteins** contain amino acids necessary for tissue maintenance. Protein is an important part of the exhaustion-prevention formula, but you can't stock up on it because any excess becomes fat. Convenient protein sources include beans, cereals, and nuts.

**Fat** is the primary way your body stores energy and proper amounts can enhance your performance. The problem is that most people store far more than necessary, and your cells don't release it for use unless you exercise extremely long and hard. Chief sources are butter, lard, cooking oil, mayonnaise, ice cream, cheese, meat, eggs, and some nuts.

Your trail diet should include no more than 50 grams of fat, compared to the 800 grams of carbohydrates and 120 grams of protein you'll need to stave off exhaustion every day. All of this provides a balanced diet of a little more than 4,000 calories, bearing in mind that calorie requirements vary depending on body size.

**Calories** fuel your body best when you're on the trail if you consume about one-fifth of them at breakfast, two-fifths during lunch and snacks, one-fifth at dinner, and the remainder in energy drinks.

It's best to eat and drink a little something each time you take a break, or at least every other break. Carbohydrates are preferable for snacks. If you wait five or six hours, then stop to stuff yourself, you're in for trouble. Dr. Paul Thomas of the University of Wyoming's Human Energy Resource Lab explains why: "Carbohydrates cause an increase in blood sugar (which gives you that energy lift). To help get this sugar into your muscles, your body produces insulin. If you eat regularly and frequently while hiking, regular amounts of insulin are produced and your body maintains its strength. If you go until you're almost empty, then load yourself with carbohydrates, your body, anticipating a flood of blood sugar, may overcompensate and create too much insulin, which causes rapid fatigue rather than rejuvenation.

"Also, carbohydrates are a good source of nutrition because fats can't be burned without them. Your body can only store about 3,000 calories of carbohydrates, so your real reserves, some 80,000 to 90,000 calories, lie in fats. The thing is, to metabolize and use them, you need the carbos."

Any sport or activity where you're told to indulge your appetite can't be all bad.

## Nutritional Needs And Habits

In a unique study, a Pennsylvania State University student named Karen Lutz examined the eating habits of long-distance hikers. She focused the study on three areas: the changes in a hiker's body composition over a long hike; the nutritive value of a typical long-distance hiker's diet; and the number of calories expended during such a trip.

Lutz set up shop one April in Amicalola Falls State Park, Georgia, along an approach trail leading to Springer Mountain, where most Appalachian Trail thru-hikers begin the long march north. She weighed the hikers, measured them all over, and determined their body fat. She also collected information on their diets, calculating calories, protein, calcium, iron, thiamine, and vitamins A and C. Then she wished them well and sent them on their way.

Lutz repeated the examinations midway between Georgia and Maine, and once more at trail's end in Baxter State Park, Maine, the northern terminus of the AT. The hikers ranged in age from 24 to 33 years old. All weighed less when they finished than when they began—an average of 20 pounds less. The smallest weight loss was eight pounds; the largest was 32.

All the hikers lost body fat, but the men lost an average of seven pounds of lean body weight and muscle tissue as well, something that's supposed to happen only when the body is under extreme physical stress. Lutz discovered this to be the norm on the trail, however. The one woman in the study was the only hiker who did not burn up lean body weight, and she even gained muscle mass. (Women's bodies have a higher ratio of fat to muscle than men, therefore a greater buffer of fat to burn before drawing on muscle tissue.)

Lutz discovered that most of the long-distance hikers ate more than 5,000 calories a day, but not a single hiker reached the 6,000-calorie level needed to maintain normal body weight. The problem is an interesting one: The more food you carry, the greater the pack weight and the more energy required to carry it. The more energy you need, the more you eat. In other words, weight loss is to be expected.

Curiously, Lutz found that hikers ate the most nutritious food halfway through their journey. Later, at the end of the trip, where they were eating greater quantities than at any other time on the trip, the nutritional value of their food choices deteriorated. Quality was sacrificed for quantity.

Using U.S. Department of Agriculture Recommended Daily Allowances as a guideline, Lutz found that protein intake generally fell within recommended levels throughout, total fat intake initially met recommended levels and then dropped steadily, and carbohydrate intake increased throughout.

Of the several nutritional failings she noted, Lutz found calcium deficiencies to be the greatest. This is supported by long-distance hikers' frequent complaints of muscle cramps, generally prevented by calcium. The hikers also suffered a deficiency of vitamin A, which is found in dark leafy greens and orange veggies that are often difficult to come by on a trail. Many hikers reported extreme sensitivity to lights while driving at night after their trip—a good indication of vitamin A deficiency.

Thiamine, a B vitamin, was also lacking significantly, which is no surprise since many favorite foods of long-distance hikers have little or no thiamine content: processed rices, pastas, and instant oatmeal. Hard physical work and stress, two factors abundant on long journeys, call for increased thiamine intake. Increased consumption of sugars and starches (carbohydrates), observed by Lutz as the miles ticked off, creates an even stronger need for thiamine, which oxidizes carbohydrates and converts them to energy.

To boost the vitamin B content in your hiking diet, try carrying rolled, unprocessed oats instead of the instant type. Soak them overnight in a pot of water and they'll cook like instant in the morning. Choose whole-grain breads and crackers instead of processed ones. Since the B vitamins are more potent if used together, it's wise to increase intake of all of them at once. Nutritional brewer's yeast, found in health-food stores, is an excellent source of these vitamins and can be carried in a small plastic bag and tossed into the evening meal.

To get more vitamin A in your diet, eat dried apricots and other fruits on a regular basis. Dates, raisins, and figs aren't extremely high in calcium, but a steady supply throughout a day increases calcium and vitamin A levels. You can further benefit by learning to identify wild edibles and greens and incorporating them into the evening stew.

Powdered milk added to various dishes, especially soups and stews at supper (make a white cream sauce), or used alone as a beverage also boosts calcium intake. Cheese is an excellent source of protein and calcium and can be carried easily for days. Oil-packed sardines, almonds, and filberts are also good sources of calcium.

## Going Vegetarian

If you're a vegetarian, you've heard it. If you're not a vegetarian, you've probably done it—that is, proclaim a vegetarian diet to be nutritionally dangerous, insufficient, or downright un-American.

The fact is, scientists have put together some impressive research indicating that the broccoli-and-tofu crowd may be less likely to die from heart disease or diabetes. Statistics also show that vegetarian men are less prone to prostate cancer, and vegetarian women have a strikingly lower incidence of breast cancer, osteoporosis, and gallstones. Not only that, but vegetarians tend to have lower blood pressure, serum cholesterol, and even body weight.

That's great news for vegetarians, and it may even persuade a few meat eaters to put away their carving knives. But will you have to leave your veggie ways behind the moment you reach the trail? Lettuce and broccoli aren't too common along most trails, and who wants to lug a weighty head of cabbage in their pack?

No problem. You merely need to know how to combine foods to get "complete protein," where all the essential amino acids (those your body cannot synthesize) are present in the best proportions. It's as simple as eating legumes and whole grains at the same meal, and it's not hard to do. Beans and rice will do. A peanut butter and jelly sandwich (peanuts are legumes) or falafel on pita bread both give you complete protein as well. Or you can nosh on soybean products like tofu (a fancy name for bean curd) and brown rice.

But how do you get these exotic dishes when tramping through the Rockies or Adirondacks? Your local outdoor store probably sells packages of vegetarian freeze-dried foods. You can also rely on backpacking staples like granola, nuts, dried fruits, and gorp.

Going totally meatless on the trail isn't for everyone, though. In fact, According to Dr. Sarah Short, one of America's foremost nutritionists, everyone should eat a little meat once in a while.

"It probably sounds like I'm against vegetarianism, but I'm not," says Dr. Short, who is something of a nutritional celebrity. She's been interviewed on TV shows like "Good Morning America" and "The Today Show," and quoted in *The New York Times*, *The Wall Street Journal*, and *Time*. "I think it's a great thing for those who want to do it, and there are certainly disadvantages to meat eating. What I am against is red-meat haters. Meat is a good source of complete protein, and the best source of well-absorbed iron and zinc. If people want to cut back on animal products, that's fine. But if you cut them out altogether, be careful about getting complete protein and enough of those other minerals."

If you do go vegetarian, Dr. Short says, eat legumes to get that crucial complete protein as well as zinc. As far as iron goes, it's poorly absorbed from vegetable sources, so throw out the idea that you merely need to eat a lot of spinach. Instead, Dr. Short says you should buy a bottle of supplements and take them regularly. While you're at it, pick up some $B_{12}$. If you're a strict vegetarian, you'll need tiny amounts of this vitamin eventually. It's not found in vegetable sources, although it is available in some fortified foods.

"I'm sort of a middle-of-the-road person," Dr. Short explains. "I believe in moderation in all things, and I hate scare tactics like, 'Eat less cholesterol or you'll die!' I also object to people cutting whole food groups from their diets. Meat is the best source of minerals. Besides, animals are being bred much leaner now, and you can pick leaner cuts."

Enjoying meatless meals in the wilderness requires a bit of planning. You don't want to tote a lot of bulky vegetables and fruits because they won't equal the calories you'll burn getting them up the trail. As for dried legumes, you'll use too much stove fuel for the lengthy boiling period required to make them edible. This is where dehydration comes in. You can buy freeze-dried or dehydrated meals—meatless, of course— in your favorite outdoor store, or you can get a food dehydrator and prepare them yourself. You can even invest in one of those gadgets that seals your food in its own boilable cooking pouch. You'll lose some of the water-soluble vitamins in the dehydration process, but it's the best way to get healthy vegetarian meals in the backcountry.

## Why Water Is So Important

Want to know why water is so vital to your trail health? About 60 to 70 percent of your body is water. About 90 percent of your blood is water. When you walk with a weighty pack on your back, your muscles heat up and perspiration occurs. The sweat evaporates on your skin's surface and cools you, allowing your bloodstream to carry cooler temperatures back to your organs, thus regulating your body's overall temperature. (To stay in good working order, your body must maintain a core temperature somewhere between 97° F to 100° F.)

Now do you understand why the cool, clear fluid is so crucial? Your heart is a pump that circulates fluid through a contained system—your body. When you don't have enough water in that system, blood thickens and it takes more pressure to push it through the vessels. Under extreme conditions, this leads to heatstroke, or what's commonly called sunstroke.

Lack of water not only increases blood pressure, it also affects your overall energy levels. When circulation slows, your blood doesn't carry carbohydrates, vitamins, and other nutrients to your tissues as effectively, so your muscles don't work as well. Replacing lost water keeps the pressure properly balanced in and out of your cells, so you metabolize nutrients efficiently and have more energy. Your kidneys need water as well, otherwise some of their workload is dumped onto your liver, slowing your metabolism even more.

Your brain and heart also need a regular flow of nutrients. When circulation is impaired, you feel it mentally and emotionally in the form of dizziness, impatience, fatigue, and confusion. Excessive panting means your heart is having trouble getting oxygen to your muscles. A headache is a classic warning sign of dehydration.

Losing and replacing water is part of your daily routine. You lose about three quarts a day through breathing, perspiration, and waste removal. Strenuous backpacking, especially in temperature extremes, causes even more water loss. So how do you know when to increase your fluid intake and by how much? The sensation of thirst doesn't accurately reflect your body's needs. You may have lost up to one percent of your body weight before the thirst signal kicks in, and the sensation of being thirsty may disappear before the lost water is replenished. The key to staying properly hydrated is to drink before you feel thirsty and keep drinking after you feel satisfied. Exact fluid needs vary from person to person. Age, physical condition, activity level, body size and degree of acclimatization all influence the amount of water you should drink each day.

As a starting point, drink at least 16 ounces of water before hitting the trail, then replenish yourself with four to six ounces every 20 to 30 minutes. To fine-tune your water needs in the field, monitor the volume and color of your urine and the frequency of urination. If you're producing clear urine at least five times a day, you're drinking enough. Cloudy or dark urine, or urination less than five times a day means you should drink more.

Here are a few important water-related tips:

• Drink a minimum of three to four quarts of water a day while hiking.

• Take extra care when hiking in humid weather. When you're dripping with sweat, you're not effectively cooled by evaporation, and overheating is more likely to occur.

• Foods supply about one-quarter of your daily water needs. That figure drops if you eat typical trail favorites like dehydrated fruits and meats.

• Avoid caffeine and alcohol. They are diuretics, which means they flush more water from your system than they add to it.

• Some antihistamines, ulcer medications, sedatives, antidepressants, tranquilizers and thyroid medicines can impair your body's heat-regulating abilities. If you're taking medication, consult your physician before hiking in hot or humid weather.

• When the sweat pours, more than water is lost. Electrolytes (sodium, chloride, potassium) are sweated out. Some commercial energy drinks offer a balanced electrolyte replacement with carbohydrates for fuel.

• Use wide-mouth water bottles. The bottoms, where bacteria can grow, are easier to clean. The bottles are fairly easy to fill in a stream. A spoon fits easily into the wide opening.

• Use clear water bottles so you can always see how much water you have left.

• Camp near water if possible, but make your camp at least 200 feet away from lakes and streams. Wash at least 100 feet from water sources. Use biodegradable soap.

## Treat Your Water Well
## And It Will Return The Favor

Hot and dusty, flushed with the romance of the wild outdoors, you hold your cup beneath a clear-blue waterfall so cold it numbs your fingers. "Just like the mountain men," you think as cup meets lips. Ahh, nature's nectar, flowing down from the high country where it was chilled by snow and ice and long winters. Taking your first sip, you toast the good life.

If you're lucky, you arise the following morning and start your day with a smile and breakfast. But if your water was alive—contaminated with all sorts of nasties you couldn't see—you start with a squat and some unsavory gut wrenching. A carefree drink of what appears to be clean, pure, mountain water, even in the most remote, pristine wilderness, can teach you an uncomfortable lesson: what you can't see *can* hurt you.

Three types of microcritters could be temporarily taking up residence in your water bottle:

**Cysts:** These hard-shelled, single-celled parasitic protozoa are the largest fluvial microorganisms, ranging in size from 5 to 15 microns. (A micron, one-millionth of a meter, equals .0000394 inches. The period at the end of this sentence measures a whopping 500 to 600 microns in diameter.) The ubiquitous Giardia cyst is responsible for most waterborne illness in the United States. *E. histolystica,* the rascal responsible for amoebic dysentery, occurs infrequently in the United States. Cryptosporidium, unknown as a cause of human illness until 1976, is becoming an increasingly common cause of gastrointestinal upset.

**Bacteria:** There are a wide variety of bacteria. A few notorious offenders: *E. coli* comes from fecal contamination and gives you the trots; *Klebsiella pneumoniae* causes, you got it, pneumonia; the various transmutations of salmonella can cause intestinal distress, fever, food poisoning, and typhoid fever; shigella can cause dysentery; staphylococcus and streptococcus both cause big, painful, pus-filled boils.

**Viruses:** These are the smallest, least pervasive waterborne fauna, but are arguably the most dangerous. Viruses cause polio and hepatitis (you can die from hepatitis B). Coxsackie and ECHO (enteric cytopathogenic human orphan) viruses are often asymptomatic but can cause diarrhea, flu, fever, and colds. Norwalk and Rota viruses also cause diarrhea. (An interesting note on these last four viruses comes from Dr. James Alexander of the federal Centers for Disease Control and Prevention in Atlanta, Georgia: "You are more likely to get them from your buddy than from backcountry water.") Viruses currently pose little danger in the surface water throughout most of the United States and Canada.

There's widespread disagreement regarding chemical pollutants in backcountry water. Some scientists say that since backpackers consume such small quantities of water for short periods of time, there's little threat. Others warn that even minimum exposure to chemicals is cause for concern. Common surface-water pollutants include diesel fuel, pesticides, and fertilizers from farmland runoff and heavy metals from mines. Better safe than sorry, so beware of water that's discolored or has an odor.

There's no practical way to know if the water at your feet contains harmful microorganisms. Backcountry water sources are living communities susceptible to sudden change, and the numbers of organisms can surge without apparent cause. Water might be safe one day and harmful the next, or it might be safe at one location and unsafe 20 yards downstream. The prudent backpacker's only choice is to purify *all* drinking water by either killing or removing the organisms. You have three options.

**1) Boiling.** There was a time when a five-minute boil was recommended for making water safe. Nowadays, it's accepted that merely bringing water to a rolling boil will do, because even the lower temperatures required to make water boil at high elevations are adequate to kill Giardia, vegetative bacteria, and viruses. Even so, the inconvenience of setting up a stove and lugging extra fuel often makes this impractical. The boiling points for high country elevations are:

| | |
|---|---|
| Sea level: | 212° F (100° C) |
| 5,000 ft.: | 203° F (95° C) |
| 10,000 ft.: | 194° F (90° C) |
| 14,000 ft.: | 187° F (86° C) |

**2) Chemical treatment.** Chlorine-based treatments, such as halazone, were once the safest chemical means for purifying water. They aren't effective against amoebic cysts, however, so most seasoned trekkers now use iodine for purification.

Whether in tablet or crystal form, iodine is light and easy to use, though its effectiveness depends on concentration of dosage, the amount of time you wait between adding iodine and drinking the water, and the water's temperature and pH. The unique odor and odd flavor of iodized water makes drinking it an acquired taste, so some people add flavored drink mixes like Tang and Kool-Aid to improve palatability. (Pregnant women and people with thyroid problems shouldn't ingest iodine.)

*Tablets:* One of the most common brands is Potable Aqua. It has a shelf life of up to five years if stored unopened at room temperature but rapidly loses effectiveness once opened, as do any iodine purifying tablets. Store tablets in an airtight bottle while on the trail. The dose is one tablet per quart of clear water at room temperature (above 50° F), then a 15-minute wait before drinking. Cloudy water or water colder than 50° F requires an additional tablet and a one-hour wait.

*Crystals:* Polar Equipment Co. makes the Polar Pure kit, which consists of a glass bottle containing a small amount of crystalline iodine, a particle trap to keep the settled crystals in the bottle, and a small thermometer on the side of the bottle that indicates when the water is safe to drink. More detailed directions are fused to the bottle so they won't rub off or be left at home. Shelf life is indefinite.

One of the newest iodine-treatment methods is a release-on-demand purifier from Water Technologies Corp. Water passes through a mesh "filter" containing iodine resin, releasing iodine on demand when microorganisms are present. You have to wait three minutes before drinking room-temperature water and half an hour for water near the freezing point. The problem is determining when the iodine content has been depleted because resin filters don't clog like carbon filters or microstrainers do. The best way to determine depletion is to notice when the unusually strong iodine taste is weak immediately after treating.

**3) *Filtering.*** Unlike boiling or chemical treatment, filtration literally cleans the water by physically straining out suspended solids, turning murky water clear. Filters also remove most, but not all, microorganisms. Some filters remove chemical impurities as well. Filters fall into two general types: gravity-fed, which relies on gravity to pull water through the filter ever so slowly; and pump-fed, where water is forced through the filter with a hand pump. The nice thing about pump models is that within the span of a few minutes you can stoop over a stream, fill your bottle, suck it dry, then fill it again before moving on.

A filter's basic task sounds simple: It removes organisms and particles. That's not easy, though, given the teensy-weensy size of the critters. It takes a very fine filter (a microstrainer) to catch them. Two types are common:

*Membrane or surface filters:* Thin sheets perforated with precisely sized holes allow water to pass easily through, while particles larger than the openings collect on the filter surface. These filters tend to clog quickly but are easy to clean and have a long service life.

*Depth filters:* Thick, porous materials such as compressed carbon or unglazed ceramic trap particles as the water moves through a complex fibrous matrix instead of blocking particles larger than a given size at the filter's surface. Depth filters can be partially cleaned by backwashing (reversing the water flow) or by brushing the outer surface. Even with regular cleaning, depth filters eventually clog and must be replaced.

The size of a filter's pores determines the organisms it can remove from water. Pore sizes are measured in microns and remember, a period is some 600 microns fat. It's unrealistic to measure all the openings in a filter element, so the most common way to determine effectiveness is to "challenge" it in a lab with water containing a known concentration of particles of a specific size and number. The result is a pore-size rating based on the size of particles that pass through the filter.

Pore-size ratings are commonly expressed as either "nominal" or "absolute." Since there is no standardized method for determining "nominal," the ratings have little value when comparing different filters. An absolute rating is just that—no particle larger than the rated size passed the filter during testing. When filter shopping, use the absolute rating as a guide.

To reliably remove the most common backcountry cootie, the Giardia cyst, a maximum pore size of four microns is recommended. Many filters have the required 0.2 micron pore size to remove bacteria as well. But because viruses can be as tiny as .0004 micron—so small they can only be seen with an electron microscope—no field device that relies solely on filtration can reliably remove them.

There's a difference between water filters and purifiers, which must be able to kill or remove bacteria, viruses, and protozoa. The only field device currently available that meets stringent Environmental Protection Agency purification standards is the PUR Explorer, which combines chemical treatment with filtration by using a resin-bound iodine element that acts as a contact disinfectant.

First Need and MSR WaterWorks brand filters contain activated carbon. Besides removing microorganisms, they eliminate a range of organic chemicals such as pesticides, herbicides, and chlorine, although they won't remove dissolved minerals such as salt. Their broad range of filtration is due to the exceptionally porous structure of carbon and "adsorption," the adhesion of molecules to a solid surface.

One key caveat regarding adsorption: There are limits to the quantity of chemicals or microorganisms a carbon filter can hold. After the threshold for a particular material is reached, the filter can no longer adequately remove that substance from that water, and previously adsorbed material can be released. For this reason manufacturers recommend replacing your carbon filters periodically, regardless of whether they show signs of clogging.

Remember, an often overlooked part of getting the best performance out of your water filter is proper cleaning, both in regular use and before long-term storage. Follow the maker's instructions carefully.

Plan your water needs before you leave home. Determine the biological and chemical hazards you may encounter, and match them with a suitable filter, disinfectant, or a combination of the two. Think before you drink, because the consequences of getting sick in the backcountry range from annoying to potentially life-threatening.

*chapter two:*

# FOOD TO EAT WHEN YOU'RE COLD, UP HIGH, OR HOT

## Food To Fight The Chill

On a short trip or in mild conditions, poor food planning can be forgiven. Most people in reasonably good shape will survive through a little hunger, malnutrition, or weight loss.

During winter, however, it's a different story. Strenuous exercise coupled with severe weather, can drain your stamina and leave you prone to frostbite, hypothermia, and other injuries. What you eat can make the difference. When it's cold outside, think of food as fuel for heat, energy, and survival.

The effects of cold can hit unexpectedly. For instance, you might find yourself ravenously hungry shortly after eating a meal. Even if you haven't exercised in that time, your body might have used up all that food just trying to keep warm. Strenuous exercise only compounds the problem. A winter activity will burn 12 percent more calories and 32 percent more fat than the same exercise done in warmer conditions.

As far as calorie requirements go, 3,000 to 4,000 calories a day usually suffice during warm-weather backpacking. In cold weather, push that to about 6,000. Maybe you've noticed that on an extended winter trip, enough food to supply you with that amount of calories is nearly impossible to carry. Even many high-mileage, long-distance summer hikers stay hungry and simply do not have the pack capacity to carry all the food they need. But it is possible, with a little knowledge and pre-planning, to ensure a safe and enjoyable trip where the bears do the growling and your stomach doesn't.

Keep two things in mind: nutrition and calories. Proteins and fats release energy over a long period of time, which makes them particularly important during long-term, strenuous activities. A piece of chocolate (carbohydrate) will give you a quick power boost for that last mountain of the day, but a hunk of cheese or a handful of jerky (fat and protein) will fuel you through a longer, less strenuous period. Proteins and fats also take a lot of energy to digest, especially at high altitudes, so they should not be eaten in large amounts before or while you're working hard. Spread them out throughout your day. A liberal use of butter in hot cereal and at supper is a good way to boost your fat intake. Dump extra powdered milk (try to get whole powdered milk instead of non-fat or low-fat) and cheese into meals to increase your protein.

Most of your calories, though, should come from relatively "instant-energy" carbohydrates, preferably complex carbohydrates like grains, pastas, instant potatoes, and dried fruits. To add extra calories and nutrients, pad your menu with foods like sunflower seeds, nuts, and raisins in your oatmeal. Drink instant soup instead of tea or coffee. Buy tuna in oil instead of low-calorie spring water. The water you use to cook your pasta is loaded with starch and carbohydrates, so use it in your meal in soups and sauces instead of discarding it. Consider the calorie-to-weight ratio of all your foods and select only those with the most calories for the least amount of weight. There is no room for "empty" food on a winter trip. Leave the featherweight NutraSweet drink mixes and Jell-O at home. A food's bulk is important here. Enough puffed rice to fill your stomach would take up half your pack.

Because water is often hard to come by on winter trips, it helps to use foods that already contain their moisture. For dessert, feast on cookies instead of instant pudding. On extended trips, canned foods or frozen homemade stews in sealed, boilable bags can cut down on water use. On longer trips, supplement meals with freeze-dried foods that take less water, require little or no cooking time, and are lightweight and compact. Rice takes less water to prepare than noodles, and skinny noodles take less fuel to cook than wide ones. One-pot meals keep hotter longer than multipart entrees, and there are fewer packages for cold fingers to open and fewer dishes to clean.

If it's painfully cold, cook twice the amount of food you expect to eat and let the leftovers freeze. In the morning, you can merely reheat and eat.

When planning a cold-weather trip, expect everything to freeze. Preslice your cheese or butter; otherwise, you'll need a saw. Oil, honey, peanut butter, jam, vinegar, sauces, and other liquids will have to be either thawed or jackhammered. In subzero weather, carry water bottles in a pocket near you or buried deep in your pack so the water won't freeze. A wool sock pulled over the bottle also offers some protection. At night, screw the lids on tight and set your bottles upside down so if ice forms, it won't plug the pouring end.

Your stove is one of the most important pieces of equipment on a winter backpacking trip. Cut a small square of closed-cell foam pad to put under your stove when cooking; it'll insulate the stove from the cold ground and decrease its heat conduction. Although it's a good idea to sleep with your stove gear anyway—to keep it warm and ready for the morning firing—white-gas models survive the abuse of cold better than others, such as the more limited butane models, which won't work at all below 20° F.

In hot weather, you cannot ignore your thirst because it's as apparent as the sweat running down your back. Cold weather, however, masks thirst because your primary concern is warmth, and the environment is far removed from the typically "thirsty" landscape—sand and searing heat. Lack of water (it's often frozen solid) usually means you drink less. But if you're hiking or skiing, you're rapidly breathing dry, cold air, which quickly dehydrates you. Dehydration can increase your risk of frostbite because your blood volume, your primary heat conductor, is actually reduced.

Tank up every time you come across running water. Drink plenty of hot drinks before and after meals to ensure consumption of that much-needed five quarts a day. When you're chilled, drink and eat hot foods to help your body warm itself. Be sure to keep liquids readily available at all times.

Don't eat snow to satisfy your thirst. It lowers your body temperature, and you expend extra energy—though you may not notice—to bring it back up. If you have to melt snow for water, have an inch or so of starter water in the pan, then slowly add snow. Use icy, crusty snow or the wettest snow available. To melt snow, you'll need to carry considerably more fuel, which, like water, weighs about two pounds per quart. You also must allow more time for meal preparations. In a brisk, cold wind, it can take an hour and a stoveful of fuel to melt and boil just one quart of water.

To keep your water supplies from freezing at night, place your tightly closed, leakproof bottles in your sleeping bag. Choose wide-mouthed containers that resist icing over. To prevent freezing during the day, cut and fit closed-cell foam pads around your water bottles as insulation. Glue the seams with contact cement.

You might also bury your water. Because snow is a good insulator, a lidded pot of water buried a foot or so under the snow will remain unfrozen overnight. Mark the spot carefully. If you are staying in one camp for several nights, bury the pot in different locations each night since snow melted around the pot produces ice.

Alcohol, often said to be a warming beverage, does create the impression of warmth by its bite and by temporarily increasing blood flow to your extremities. But this only serves to rob your body core of much-needed heat and on the whole, drops your body temperature. Avoid caffeine, too, which constricts blood vessels and is a diuretic.

Everyone reacts differently to the cold, depending on metabolism, body size, gender, normal body temperature, and health. Smaller people have more body surface for their weight than bigger people, so they lose heat more easily. Women's body temperatures run three to four degrees lower than men's, and their hands and feet are more prone to feeling cold sooner.

Of particular importance to women is the role iron plays in resisting cold. Iron assists the formation of hemoglobin, an oxygen-carrier important for heat-producing processes. A deficiency in iron can alter thyroid metabolism, which regulates body heat. Because most women are iron deficient, they should consider taking iron supplements. You can also add foods like molasses, wheat germ, and apricots to a winter backpacking diet to boost iron intake. Eat vitamin C-rich foods simultaneously to enhance iron absorption. Because your body is coldest between 3 A.M. and 5 A.M., take a high-iron, high-calorie snack to bed with you in case you wake up hungry and cold.

When it comes down to it, aside from the peace and stark beauty of the winter landscape, cold-weather backpacking is one of the few times you can eat a lot, run clear off the caloric chart, and not gain weight or feel guilty. That, in itself, is a treat!

### COLD-WEATHER MENU GUIDELINES

**Breakfast:** Quick and simple breakfasts speed up cold, early morning departures. The dry ingredients can be mixed at home and sealed in plastic bags. Try a hot porridge or oatmeal mixed with granola and whole milk, and hot drinks. Add dried fruit or cinnamon and nutmeg to the mush. Accompany it with a hot drink.

¾ cup quick-cooking rolled oats
1 cup granola
½ cup powdered milk
¼ cup dried fruit
1 Tbsp. cinnamon and nutmeg

Boil 1½ cups water and stir in dry ingredients. Cover and let sit a few minutes. Makes one serving.

**Lunch:** Start with high-energy snack foods.

1 chocolate bar
1 snack bar

Then dig into dried fruit, meats, cheese, and sugary foods such as:

cookies
granola bars
salami
candy
jerky
cheese
pepperoni
gorp

Move on to a "main course."

2 bagels with cream cheese
or substitute ⅛ loaf logan bread
or crackers with cheese
avocado
½ cup sprouts

**Dinner:** Go for one-pot simplicity. Freeze-dried package dinners are convenient but you can eat homemade as well. Select from the usual starch staples or try tortillas or dumplings. At home, mix everything—sauces, dried vegetables, seasonings, or oils—in a plastic bag. Hot drinks and instant soups before dinner keep up fluids and body heat.

1½ cups pasta
1 cup elbow macaroni
1 cup instant brown rice
1 cup instant rice
1 cup seasoned rice
1 cup potato flakes
½ cup powdered milk for potatoes
1 package Ramen noodles

Choose one starch each day. From there, add protein: meat, cheese, nuts, soynuts or flakes, and any of a variety of seeds. Makes one serving.

**The Goodie Bag:** Dip into this reserve if you think a meal needs something more. Here's where you keep cheeses, spices (tamari powder or sauce, ginger root, cinnamon, and nutmeg), and salt, sweeteners, coffee, tea, soups, cocoa, powdered milk, desserts, fats and oils, and any other perishables.

## Nutritional Needs When You're Way Up There

Altitude. The word conjures visions of cold air whistling over rocky peaks and clouds swirling overhead as you labor through a high pass. Even if you have all the right gear to travel through such a landscape, the seemingly simple task of cooking and eating can be an unexpected challenge. For wilderness trips in moderately high elevations of 7,000 to 14,000 feet, heights most backpackers reach at one time or another during their travels, knowledge of how altitude affects your body, nutritional needs, and food preparation can make a big difference in whether or not your trip's a success.

It all starts with air. No matter what the altitude, the air you breathe is 21 percent oxygen. At sea level, the huge weight of the atmosphere above compresses more oxygen into each lungful. But at higher elevations where the air is less dense, the amount of oxygen per breath is smaller, and the low pressure slows the oxygen's movement across lung membranes into your bloodstream. This is why even fit people sometimes do poorly at high altitude. The lack of oxygen makes it difficult for tissues to store and release energy and produce heat.

A string of conditions accompany altitude. For one thing, it's colder up there. Temperatures drop about 3.5° F for every 1,000-foot rise in elevation. For another, the slopes may rise more steeply, so you work harder to remain warm on hills that are more difficult to navigate. You'll find yourself tired without a clue as to how you drained your reserves. You may have a headache, shortness of breath, lethargy, nausea, lost appetite, and feelings of exhaustion.

You might think a good meal would give you energy and boost your spirits. But altitude can straitjacket your appetite, especially during the early days of being up high. So while you sit there tired and in desperate need of a meal, you aren't interested in eating. Unless you overcome this lack of appetite, your body will start breaking down its fats and proteins for energy, an inefficient process that further drains you.

You can't prevent the conditions that make altitude so difficult, but you can prepare for them. Drinking a lot of water is your first defense. The increased volume and rate of breathing, combined with the dry, cold air, dramatically increases fluid loss. In the mountains, you can lose an additional two quarts of water each day just breathing. Add a heavy pack to that mountain trek and you can lose half a quart or more each hour. If you don't feel thirsty enough to drink much at one sitting, drink smaller portions at frequent intervals.

If you're hiking above 7,000 feet, add an additional two or three quarts of water per day to maintain normal hydration. If your high altitude activities are strenuous (carrying a heavy pack over difficult terrain), you should drink three or more additional quarts a day. If you go above 12,000 feet, guzzle with abandon, perhaps as much as five to seven additional quarts daily.

A steady supply of food energy is just as important. Since your decreased appetite can make this difficult, the next-best thing is to increase the caloric values of your meal portions.

You'll meet your high-altitude energy needs most efficiently if you mix the basic food components in these caloric proportions: 60 to 70 percent carbohydrates, 10 to 20 percent proteins, and 15 to 25 percent fats. None of these three energy sources can stand alone. Fatty foods like butter, cheese, nuts, and cooking oils, although high in calories, can cause poor digestion and diarrhea if you eat too much of them. High protein foods like meats, eggs, fish, and legumes provide essential nutrients, but require a lot of time to break down during digestion. Carbohydrates like rice, pasta, potatoes, bread, candies, fruits, and vegetables are easily broken down and used, but don't provide long-lasting sources of energy.

No matter how much you eat at a sitting, three meals a day may not keep you satisfied. Snack frequently between meals, and definitely consider taking vitamin-mineral supplements to ensure complete nutrition. Iron has been shown to be especially important for producing heat in cold weather.

As if being tired, grumpy, and without an appetite weren't bad enough, cooking at altitude becomes more difficult. Low atmospheric pressure at high altitudes means water boils at a lower temperature, so it never gets particularly hot. In other words, it takes longer to cook things, which can make you even grumpier. You should plan to spend more time cooking and expect to use more stove fuel than usual.

There is one way around this, though. If your group size is large enough to justify the extra weight, a small backpacking pressure-cooker will compensate for altitude and reduce cooking times by raising the pressure and water temperature. Decreasing cooking time saves you fuel, too. Two-and-a-half-quart to four-quart pressure cookers made of aluminum work well. Look for models with side grips instead of extended saucepan-type handles to ease packing. Pressure settings typically range from five to 15 pounds; the most versatile cookers feature more than one setting. Incidentally, salted water does not boil at a significantly higher temperature.

For travel above 7,000 feet, choose your stove carefully. Alcohol and butane perform poorly, but white gas, kerosene, and propane provide very hot flames. Your stove's windscreen will improve heat transfer.

Your trusty grocery store is a good source of foods that do well at higher elevations. Shop for quick-cooking pasta, potato or rice dishes, powdered sauce mixes, "skillet" dinners, canned and dehydrated meats, dried fruits, nuts, hot cereals, cheeses, and desserts. The natural-foods section is worth a look, too.

Glancing at our sample day's menu, you'll see some freeze-dried foods listed. However, unless weight is a major factor, consider dehydrated, dried, canned, or fresh products. These take longer to cook but generally taste better, so you'll eat more. Consider retort foods (flexible aluminum packages of complete, precooked meals that can be heated in boiling water, often available through military-surplus suppliers) or complete freeze-dried dinners for days when the weather grumbles or exhaustion overcomes the will to cook.

Like the mountains you'll be feasting atop, high altitude cooking is a large topic. But with these basic tools and principles, you will be able to avoid a lot of problems and maybe even enjoy turning away from the vistas briefly to stir the pot.

### SAMPLE HIGH-ALTITUDE MENU

**Breakfast:**
juice from crystals
freeze-dried sausage patties

scrambled powdered eggs
hash brown potatoes from dehydrated flakes
milk
hot drink (eggnog, cider, or herb tea)

**Midmorning Snack:**
dried fruits
nuts, cookies, or granola bars
fruit juices

**Lunch:** For on-the-trail eating, consider a cold meal.
cheese spreads and crackers
canned kippered snacks
clams or oysters
beef jerky
fruit leather or pemmican
juice from crystals or water

If you are in camp, you can prepare a hot meal.
soup
crackers
macaroni and cheese
cookies
beverage

**Midafternoon Snack:**
juice from crystals or other beverage
sliced brown bread
cheese or nut-butter spreads

**Dinner:** This meal can be hot since you're in camp.
hot consomme or bouillon
brown rice
shrimp Newburg
canned three-bean salad (or freeze-dried vegetable)
no-bake cheesecake or mousse dessert

## Keeping Cool When The Temperature Rises

Planning for hot-weather hiking usually means minimizing your exposure to the heat. Hike in the morning and evening (even at night!), and rest in the shade at midday. Wear industrial strength sunblock, a wide-brimmed hat, and good sunglasses when in the sun. Wear light-colored cotton apparel.

In the heat, water intake should always be on your mind. In hot or desert conditions, a gallon of water a day per person is minimum. Strenuous hiking in hot weather can increase the rate of water loss to as much as three quarts an hour. If you're planning to find water, make certain your information and maps are reliable and current.

It's better to carry your own water using one- and two-liter bottles. If you put all your fluid in a single large jug and it leaks, you've got a full-blown catastrophe on your hands. Besides, your load will carry better with smaller bottles. The weight of water (nine pounds a gallon with bottles) sounds like a logistical nightmare, but it's not as bad as it sounds because in hot weather you'll be carrying less gear.

Take food, for example. On a winter trip, your pack is stuffed with tons of food, a stove and fuel bottles, and lots of clothes. But appetites usually drop in the heat, so go aboriginal. Have a cold breakfast and skip the stove. Forget the cook kit and eat finger foods, and drink fruit juices all day.

There's that word "drink" again. As if the importance of fluid consumption hasn't been emphasized enough, here's another reason to drink at every opportunity—to prevent what are broadly referred to as heat emergencies. Normally, sweating regulates your core body temperature. But sometimes we sweat faster than we replenish our water supply. Problems start if we run low on body water or if the humidity level is so high that evaporation stops. Your core body temperature may rise, which is a potentially disastrous situation.

Lose too much fluid, and it causes thicker blood flow, which impedes your body's ability to maintain a safe temperature. If your internal heat regulating mechanisms break down completely, your body can't cool itself and you're likely to suffer heatstroke. Symptoms include goosebumps on your body and upper arms, a chilled feeling, a throbbing pressure in your head, nausea, weakness, and dry skin when you know you should be sweating. Hyperthermia, if ignored, can even kill you.

To avoid these symptoms, drink plenty of cool liquids

before and during strenuous physical activity in hot or humid conditions. Drink about one cup every 15 minutes during prolonged exercise. On a hike, this may mean prearranging water storage drop-offs or finding adequate water holes. If you can't plan for proper water supplies, cancel your hike.

If you notice symptoms of dehydration and heat exhaustion, rest in the coolest place you can find. Drink cool water. Don't try to keep going. Remember that serious dehydration and hyperthermia require expert medical attention, with the treatment often including the administration of intravenous fluids and ice-water baths. Since you won't find these in the field, stop before it's too late.

As for the Big Question—how long can I survive without water?—it depends on the temperature and your activity. According to William Forgey, M.D., author of *Wilderness Medicine:*

• At 120° F, with no water available, you'll last about two days, regardless of your activity level. With four quarts, you may live two days longer.

• At 90° F, with no water, you might make it five days if you travel only during the day, or seven days if you travel at night or not at all. With four quarts of water, you could survive 6½ days traveling by day and 10 days traveling by night. With 10 quarts, your odds of survival increase to eight days and 15 days, respectively.

• At 60° F, you could survive eight days with no water if you're active or 10 days if you're inactive.

*chapter three:*
# JUST ADD WATER

## Freeze-Dried Food—Nutrition In A Pouch

Outdoor cooking is charmed. No matter what sort of glop you throw together after a day of sucking trail dust, it usually tastes good, even when it tastes bad. This axiom helps explain our 40-year, stormy romance with freeze-dried food, that arid mixture in a pouch that has become such a staple of outdoor life. To most people, freeze-dried remains the mysterious product of some arcane wizardry. Is it food as we know it? Am I really "eating"?

Contrary to what some backpackers claim, freeze-dried food is food. The process of drawing water (actually ice) out of frozen food under a vacuum leaves the nutrients remarkably undisturbed. Only trace amounts of important vitamins like B and C are lost, partly because these are water soluble. The nutritive value of essential amino acids and proteins remains largely intact as well. And unlike dehydrated foods, the cell walls are unaltered in the freeze-drying process, so the products look similar to unprocessed foods—well, sort of. Some folks claim you can identify the ingredients in their freeze-dried entrees before cooking by simply poking and looking. Well, maybe.

Food quality and taste have radically changed in the past few years. In the old days, it didn't matter what freeze-dried meal you ate because by dinner's end you were certain that you'd tasted the same thing before. Several times. Daniel Boone Ricey Beans, General Custer Eggs, Squatting Turkey Soup—it all tasted like Musha Goulash.

It all tasted the same for a good reason: Most freeze-dried foods were prepared with the same heavy preservatives, salts, and flavor enhancers, particularly monosodium glutamate (MSG). But these days, most manufacturers avoid preservatives, MSG, and artificial colorings.

There has been a growing trend toward natural products as well. With advances in technology, manufacturers are able, in most cases, to eliminate artificial ingredients while improving taste and extending shelf life. In other cases, the additives have been trimmed.

Variety is also a new factor. Besides the regular meat-and-potatoes dishes most of America grew up on, there are now exotic international, gourmet, and "health food" meals, plus more meatless entrees. The majority of these meals are instant—no cooking! Just add boiling water and let sit. They require little water and fuel, and weigh next to nothing. But they can be expensive.

When shopping for freeze-dried foods and planning your menu, keep a few points in mind:

• One company's entrees may fill two people who are out for an easy weekend hike, but a hard-driving, long-distance hiker, whose body fat has disappeared, will be left hungry from that same selection.

• Desert hikers and mountain climbers may need all no-cook meals that use little water.

• Consider less expensive dehydrated food if you have lots of time to sit and stir and watch the sun set.

• Meat entrees are considerably more expensive than meatless, with seafood even more so.

• Always check how much food an entree makes. A cheaper meal may be lighter on your pocketbook, but then it might sit lighter in your stomach, too.

Freeze-dried food probably will never match the taste, cost, nutrition, and emotional satisfaction of making your own meal. But the combination of light weight, easy preparation, preservability, new tastes, and conscientious nutrition makes freeze-dried a valuable part of the backpacking kitchen.

## WHAT WOULD THE OLD-TIMERS HAVE THOUGHT?

John Muir, who spent every free minute tramping through his beloved Sierras in California, knew the secret of traveling light. He carried bread and tea in his pockets on long hikes in the mountains. What would Muir think of today's backpackers toting along shrimp creole, ham Romanoff, or beef amandine?

John Wesley Powell, the one-armed major, ran 1,000 miles of the Green and Colorado rivers in 1864. His provisions: beans, salt, bacon, flour, coffee, dried apples, tea, rice, and sugar. He couldn't "just add boiling water."

Clarence King, exploring Sierra Nevada peaks and valleys during Powell's era, relied heavily on fresh venison, beans, and flour. How long has it been since a backpacker asked at the camping store for a 50-pound sack of flour?

The famous Sourdough Expedition of 1913, which was basically a bunch of Alaskan prospectors on a lark, ascended to the lower of Mt. McKinley's two summits. While modern-day expeditions spend weeks moving their camps, including great quantities of lightweight food, ever higher on the mountain until they are in a position to make a summit bid, such tenderfoot precautions were not for the Sourdoughs! One fair day, they left their base camp at 11,000 feet and climbed to within 300 feet of the 20,300-foot summit of North America, and descended to their base. And their food? A picnic lunch, basically.

### Dry Your Own Food At Home

Freeze-dried fare and commercially dehydrated foods may burden your pocketbook when you're planning a backpacking menu. Fortunately, anyone can dry vegetables, fruits, and meats at home for a fraction of the cost. And you don't even need to buy a dehydrator because your oven will do the trick.

Impatient types beware, you'll need a full day for this project. But in the end, as you enjoy a sunset feast on the trail, chances are you'll have a little more emotional connection to your home-dried food.

First, you need a drying rack. This can be a small wooden produce crate or a cardboard box with slits cut in it. The surface of the rack used to hold the foods should be lined with cheesecloth. Select good quality, fully ripe fruits and vegetables. Slice them into strips about ⅛ inch thick; thicker strips will take longer to dry.

Before drying, **fruits and vegetables** must be blanched (preheated) to destroy enzymes that could cause your dried foods to rot. One blanching method is to steam the food for a few minutes. Arrange the slices loosely in a steamer (you can also use a wok or a colander set inside a covered pot) so the steam circulates well. The food is sufficiently blanched when it looks cooked and is limp. Blanching time for most green vegetables and tomatoes is about three minutes; for most fruits, about six minutes. Pineapples, peaches, and nectarines take about 10 minutes. Potatoes take about seven minutes.

Once blanching is complete, place the foods on a towel and blot them dry, then place them on the drying rack, leaving a small space between each piece. Place the drying rack in an oven preheated to between 120° F and 140° F. If your oven doesn't have a setting that low, leave the door slightly ajar and monitor the proper heat with an oven thermometer. Heat for drying must come from below the rack. If you use an electric oven with an upper heating element that heats at low temperatures, disconnect it prior to drying your food.

After the food has dried for four hours, turn it over. Most fruits and vegetables will be thoroughly dried in eight hours. Juicier fruits may take a little longer. Dried fruits and vegetables should be firm but not hard or moist. If you can squeeze moisture out of the foods, they need more drying. If they are brittle, they have dried too much.

To further preserve your dried food, place it in a closed oven set at 175° F for 15 minutes. Let the food cool, then put in plastic bags and store in a cool, dark place.

Making meat **jerky** is easier than drying fruits and vegetables. Choose a good grade of lean beef (venison, chicken, turkey, or ham will work, too). Remove as much fat as possible and cut the beef into ¼- to ½-inch strips. Be sure to cut with the grain of the meat. Strip width is a matter of personal preference, although thinner strips dry more quickly.

After blotting the meat to remove moisture, sprinkle salt and spices on both sides, then dry in the oven as you would for fruits and vegetables. After about five hours drying per side, the jerky should be done. It will look dark and shriveled but should be chewy, not brittle. After the jerky has cooled, store in plastic bags at room temperature. Jerky with excess fat on it should be stored in a freezer.

On the trail, dried fruit and jerky make great instant snacks or can be worked into your bigger meal plans. Dried vegetables are best rehydrated. When you stop for the day, your first task should be to put the evening's dried veggies in a pot of water to soak. You can also put the dinner veggies in a full water bottle in the morning so they'll be plump and ready to go at day's end.

## DEHYDRATED TRAIL FOODS

**Baby fruit leather:** Smear fruit baby food ¼ inch thick over a cookie sheet. Set in oven at 150° F with the oven door ajar for eight hours. Remove from pan, cut into strips and roll.

**Fruit leather:** If you're feeling a little too grown up for baby food, almost any fruit can be made into leather. Berries, peaches, apricots, and rhubarb are good.

Wash the fruit, pit or remove seeds, and cut out any discolorations, but do not peel. Puree in a blender with about two tablespoons water until you have two cups of fruit puree. Season to taste by blending in sugar or honey. Line a cookie sheet with heavy plastic wrap (not foil) fastened with masking tape to the outside bottom of the pan. Spread puree evenly and dry six to eight hours in the hot sun or in a 150° F to 180° F oven. While still warm, remove from sheet, peel off plastic, and lay on a clean sheet of wrap or waxed paper. Roll and store in a cool, dry place.

**Tomato leather:** Tired of carrying cans of tomato sauce? Try spreading your cookie sheet with tomato paste and dry as above. Tomato leather reconstitutes easily, and you can leave the cans behind.

**Dehydrated ground meats:** Lean ground beef, chicken, turkey, or ham may be used. Fry meat briefly to remove excess fat and water. Chicken and turkey can be baked or stewed, then ground and dried. Spread ground meat on rack and dry in a 150° F to 180° F oven for six to eight hours. Store in plastic bags, one cup to each bag, and freeze. Add to stews, casseroles, etc., or eat as trail food.

**Dried apples:** Core apples, peel them if you like, and slice no thicker than ¼ inch. Spread on your drying rack and air dry for several days, turning occasionally, or place in a 150° F to 180° F oven for six to eight hours. Seven pounds of fresh apples makes about one pound of dried. Peaches and nectarines also can be dried this way.

**Sweet parched corn:** Cut the kernels off fresh garden corn. Let kernels dry overnight in wide flat pan. Place pan in a 300° F to 350° F oven and parch corn until light brown. Sprinkle evenly with two or three tablespoons brown sugar and heat again until the sugar melts. Cool mixture, and grind in a food grinder. Store in a tin or plastic bag. Eat as trail food or to supplement meals. A pound of fresh corn reduces to about ½ pound when dried.

### DO-IT-YOURSELF DEHYDRATED DINNERS

#### *Spanish Rice*

Start by dehydrating the following:
>        1 can (8 oz.) tomato sauce
>        1 can (16 oz.)corn
>        1 can (6 oz.) mushrooms
>        ½ chopped onion
>        ½ lb. ground jerky

Combine the dehydrated ingredients with a box of Minute Rice and two tablespoons of taco seasoning. Reconstitute with four cups of water and cook 30 minutes.

#### *Chicken And Noodles*

Dehydrate the following:
>        ½ lb. ground chicken for jerky
>        ½ cup chopped onion

To the dehydrated ingredients, add:
1 pkg.cream of mushroom soup mix
8 oz. whole wheat noodles

Reconstitute with three cups of water. Cook for 45 minutes.

## The Advantages Of Supermarket Provisions

Let us consider the following radical trail concept: Traveling light is not always the most important thing. Blasphemy! But read on anyway.

We all know the benefits of freeze-dried food. It's light, it's easy to prepare, and there's little chance of it spoiling in your pack. It's the tried-and-true way to dine on the trail. Fine.

But what if you have the option of dining on food that tastes almost home-cooked, adds a negligible amount of extra weight to your pack, and is about half the price of conventional, prepackaged trail meals? Got you interested, right?

It may take a bit more time and effort, but simple grocery-store provisions can be deliciously worthwhile. A carefully planned stroll down the store aisles will reveal a surprising variety of dry or dehydrated foods, with weight and longevity to suit your trip.

**Breakfast:** Cereals with powdered milk are a natural choice to save space in the pack (granola, muesli, quick or instant oatmeal, GrapeNuts, Cream of Wheat, and the like). Their freshness will easily outlast your hike. Cooked breakfast cereals warm body and soul, but adding hot powdered milk to almost any cereal produces the same effect. To enhance a cereal's palatability and nutrition, add Instant Breakfast.

It may sound strange, but instant potatoes with butter serve up a delicious and nutritious hot breakfast. Eggs in dried bulk form and instant western omelette mixes are good, but fresh eggs will last for two or three days if kept relatively cool in a container that prevents breakage. Be sure to pack some margarine in a tube or tub for the cooking pan. If you don't want to cook, try any of the "breakfast bars" available.

If possible, keep eggs below 50° F. Margarine will not spoil if kept below room temperature, or 75° F. In general, salmonella poisoning can occur when foods are stored at room temperature (70° F and higher), and particularly in high humidity. Double-bagging, foil-wrapping, and storing foods at the center of your pack will help keep them cool, even when midday temperatures rise. When possible, dunk bagged foods into a mountain stream to lower their temperatures before going on with the rest of your day's itinerary.

If the weather will not cooperate with your foods' temperature requirements, consider alternatives like powdered butter salt and powdered eggs. You'll sacrifice a bit of taste, but these foods keep under difficult conditions.

Don't forget instant coffee, hot chocolate, and tea bags because nothing beats a hot drink as you watch the high-country frost melt.

**Lunch:** Peanut butter and jelly on pita or bread is a classic. Store creamy condiments like nut butters or liquid margarine in reusable plastic squeeze tubes available at outdoor shops, or in plastic tubs from grocery stores. Be sure to double-bag them to contain the inevitable drips. Bread must be dense (like pita, pumpernickel, and rye) so it doesn't squash or take up excess space, and tough so it doesn't crumble. English muffins and bagels hold up well, though they're a little bulky.

Cheese is a staple, but seal it well so the oil that separates in a warm pack doesn't dribble all over. Avoid sharp cheeses, which can turn almost liquid in hot weather. Plastic-pouched lunch meats work, too, if you can stand the preservatives. Pepperoni and salami are old standbys. Again, pack them tightly, and watch out for spoilage.

**Snacks:** Dried fruits make a welcome dessert at any meal, and invariably become snacks. Many supermarkets have barrels stocked full of long-lasting fruits, nuts, and other munchables that you can buy in bulk—cheaper than paying for prepackaged gorp. Some grocery stores sell fruit leathers that are even more compact than whole dried fruits and just as tasty. On the trail, you'll need these snacks to keep your energy up.

Lots of people pack hard candies or chocolate bars for

quick energy boosts, though the nutritional value is questionable. If nothing else, they are morale boosters if you can ignore what they are doing to your teeth.

**Dinner:** For their simplicity and nutrition, casseroles epitomize backpacking dinner entrees. Here, the grocery-store backpacker is in luck, because many supermarkets feature an entire aisle of dried, boxed casseroles. Many come close to matching the weight and bulk of freeze-dried, but you'll often have to add your own meat or cheese to get the nutrition and flavor you need.

You can easily make up your own casserole with noodles, rice, beans, peas, grains, pilafs, or cheeses. Just use the dried versions of ingredients listed in your kitchen cookbook. Powdered sauce mixes are available to make spaghetti, tacos, chili, stroganoff, sour cream, pesto, cheese, and even cooking wine. Mix the dry ingredients at home to save time later.

If your casserole becomes too watery, call it a soup or stew and enjoy it. The bulkier, often starchier prepackaged soups work great as a hot liquid to tide you over while dinner simmers, but most are low in nutrition, despite the healthy-looking labels. Also, beware of MSG, a flavor enhancer commonly found in supermarket dried foods. Don't find out that you react to the stuff (with vague, hangover-like symptoms) midway through a week-long trip.

Some healthy lightweight foods, like dried beans, are notorious for long-simmering preparation times that require lots of fuel. Soaking them in water in a bag tied to your pack while you hike cuts the cooking time in half. To help avoid the morning-after flatulence, try eating whole-grain rice or bread with your beans.

Tomato sauce forms a base for many meals: spaghetti, rice mixes, stew, egg concoctions. Use a powdered form or tomato paste that you can thin with water while cooking. For a long trip, transfer the paste to a plastic tube.

For vegetable fillers, the spice rack provides alternates to some fresh items: dried onion flakes, garlic, parsley, celery, green peppers, and mushrooms. These can also liven up soups, stews, and breakfast eggs. Fresh onions, carrots, cauliflower, and cabbage pack and preserve well on the trail if you can handle the weight. For an easy side salad, soak chopped portions of these in a little water and eat them raw. Powdered potatoes may not sound especially appetizing for dinner at home, but 20 miles in the bush, you'll find the potatoes—with some margarine, salt, pepper, onion flakes, garlic powder, or parsley—downright delicious.

For the carnivorous, smoked meats such as bacon, sausage and ham will keep for several days on the trail. Still, use them up early in your itinerary. Beef jerky can be easily substituted for beef or hamburger in casseroles, and it reconstitutes easily in a little boiling water.

## SAMPLE SUPERMARKET-TRIP MENU

| | Breakfast | Lunch | Dinner |
|---|---|---|---|
| Day 1 | eat at home | meat sticks<br>granola bars<br>fruit drink<br>gum | scalloped<br>  potatoes<br>  w/ham<br>instant pea soup<br>cookies<br>milk |
| Day 2 | French toast<br>  w/syrup<br>fried ham<br>spiced cider<br>coffee | cheese sandwiches<br>instant soup<br>nuts and raisins<br>fruit drink<br>milk | beef/rice<br>  casserole<br>vegetable<br>rye crackers<br>instant pudding<br>fruit drink |
| Day 3 | bacon<br>eggs<br>  w/dill, onion,<br>  and cheese<br>orange drink | pasta salad<br>instant soup<br>dried apricots<br>fruit drink<br>milk | pepperoni<br>  spaghetti<br>Parmesan cheese<br>garlic toast<br>cookies<br>coffee or cocoa |

|  | **Breakfast** | **Lunch** | **Dinner** |
|---|---|---|---|
| Day 4 | oatmeal w/cinnamon, raisins, and brown sugar spiced cider coffee milk | peanut butter and jelly sandwiches instant soup dates fruit drink | beef Stroganoff vegetable rye crackers instant pudding milk |
| Day 5 | pancakes w/syrup stewed mixed fruit coffee/cocoa | spinach tortellini Parmesan cheese dried apple slices chicken bouillon orange drink | meatless chili pasta salad rye crackers instant pudding milk |
| Day 6 | granola milk spiced cider coffee | granola bars meat sticks trail mix fruit drink gum | eat at home |

## TIPS FOR PACKAGING AND PREPARING FOOD

• Remove grocery-store food from its commercial package and repack (along with instructions) in tough, freezer-durable, zip-top plastic bags. Pack whole meals together so you won't need to rummage later. Double-bag large quantities of powders in case one bag springs a leak.

• Fresh eggs or other fragile items can be packed with a minimum of wasted space in those cylindrical canisters stacked potato chips come in. Cushion the eggs with paper towels, toilet tissue, marshmallows, or oatmeal.

• Tired of eating everything with a spoon? Bring along a fork, but try cutting off part of your utensil handles to save space and weight. Same goes for your toothbrush. Now everything will fit into your cooking pot.

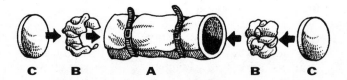

C      B      A      B      C

• If you want to take meat, ice cubes, or other perishables on a hot-weather hike, try making your own portable cooler. Gather together your closed-cell foam pad, wads of newspaper, and some extra closed-cell foam, then, put the food, ice, or whatever in a plastic bag and seal. Place the bag on the foam pad, roll the pad up, and tie the roll closed (A). Stuff leftover space with wads of newspaper (B). Finally, cut round discs from the extra foam to seal each end of the roll (C).

• To make finding your food easy, create a packing plan. For instance, label each meal with the day it's to be eaten. Put all your breakfast items in one stuff sack, your lunch items in another, your dinner food in a third, and snacks in a fourth. Label the sacks, then all you have to do at mealtime is grab the right bag.

• Tired of having your butter leak or turn rancid? Carry clarified butter (water, curd and whey are removed). It won't spoil. Unheated, it tastes lousy, but cook, bake, fry, or simply heat it and it's great. Actually, you probably recognize the flavor—it's used on commercial popcorn.

• Got the dishwashing blues? Try no-dish food preparation. Buy foods that can be reconstituted with water, prepackage your meals in quart-sized resealable bags, and carry a quart-sized plastic cup or bowl on the trail. At mealtime, boil water and simply pour it into the bag. Most of these baggies can withstand 170° F, but many will hold water that's 212° F if the bag is supported—in this case, set it in the bowl. Stir the contents, zip the bag closed, and let sit for about five minutes. Obviously, you can use the same system with foods that require only cold water. Freeze-dried food can be used. To reduce the time it takes to reconstitute, run it through a blender at home before bagging. The smaller pieces will absorb the water faster and reduce waiting time.

• Waterproof your matches by dipping the heads in liquid wax. Small, plastic pill bottles make excellent match carriers.

For a striker, cut a piece of rough sandpaper to fit the inside of the cap and glue it in place.

• An aluminum pie tin makes an inexpensive, lightweight frying pan. It's not hard to clean if done right away with hot water. It can also double as a pot lid.

## Hang It High—Protect Your Food From Bears

You're not the only hungry animal in the wilderness. Bears, squirrels, chipmunks, and other varmints are as aware of your food as you are. To save your meals and ensure your safety, hang your food when you're in the backcountry.

It's likely you can fend off a starving chipmunk, but black bears (*Ursus americanus*), widespread throughout the Appalachians, Rockies and Sierra, are another matter. Bears are intelligent and learn quickly, and they will eat anything you do. When they repeatedly obtain human food or garbage, the rewards overwhelm their natural fear of people, and they can become quite persistent. If a bear turns destructive and potentially dangerous, it will be destroyed by park authorities. But bears are the park residents, and we are only visitors; it's our responsibility to keep the bears from becoming problems.

The counterbalance hanging technique keeps most black bears and other wildlife from enjoying your meals before you do. The technique involves two food sacks of equal weight hanging in balance over the end of a high tree branch. It sounds simple but it takes practice.

Counterbalance preparation starts with your campsite choice; tree availability, not access to water or aesthetics, determines the site. You'll need to make camp early because you'll need time to eat, clean up, and still have enough daylight to play the food-hanging game. Try it from the light of a flashlight and you'll need extra-large helpings of skill, patience, and good humor.

Besides food, hang everything that holds odors, such as shampoo, soap, insect repellent, sunscreen, and water bottles containing drink mix. Don't forget about wooden spoons, the pot scrubber, garbage, and snacks stored in fannypacks. Leave your empty pack on the ground with the top flap and pockets open so the bear won't tear it apart during his search. Store water bottles out of sight since bears will test any container.

Ideally, the sacks shouldn't exceed 10 pounds each, but on an extended trip, that may be impossible. The heavier the bags, the more difficult counterbalancing becomes. A carabiner helps fasten multiple drawcords together and eliminates knots, which often come loose. The trick comes in getting both bags the same distance from the ground. Weight the bags evenly and adjust their hanging height with a long stick.

After completing your best hanging job, set up the tent a few yards from the suspended sacks but not directly underneath; you don't want to find bear and sacks in bed with you if they fall. Position a tent window in direct view of the hanging food. Your close proximity will do nothing to keep bears away, but it will let you hear them arrive.

Assemble an arsenal of small rocks by each tent's exit—more than a few, because repeated night raids are common. Arrange your (clean!) cook gear around the base of the tree and on the ground below the sacks as a burglar alarm. The clanging metal should wake you before the sound of food bags hitting the ground does. Put the lightest sleeper by the window or door, and sleep with one ear open.

All this might sound pretty bearproof, but these camp robbers can be surprisingly ingenious. If the branch is too strong a bear can walk out, pull up your rope, and chew it until the sacks drop. If the limb is too springy, bears can bounce sacks off the end. A mother might even send a cub out to retrieve the loot. If a bear does score, remember that it's your responsibility to clean up his mess.

If it's beginning to sound like you can't win, then you're finally getting the picture. Carla Neasel, one of five Yosemite rangers hired to roam the park's backcountry and educate visitors on proper food storage, says, "Consider hanging your food as a delaying tactic only. It merely buys you enough time to get up and act."

In the high country, the absence of suitable bear-bagging trees poses a challenge. You might try suspending your food sacks over a rock face by jamming the cordlock into a crack reached from above. You could hang it off a ledge safe enough for nimble humans but not clumsy bears.

There are such things as portable bearproof food canisters, but they're fairly expensive and usually heavy.

Individual parks with varying bear species suggest different ways of dealing with robber bears. In 1987, Yosemite, Sequoia, and Kings Canyon national parks adopted a "mild aggression" policy, in which they encouraged campers to bang pots, yell, and throw objects in hopes of restoring black bears' natural, human-avoiding behavior. One bit of advice: Never aim at a bear's face because a direct facial hit might provoke an angry charge. Throw to sting, not to injure, then back off to give the bear room.

Grizzly bears (*Ursus arctos horribilis*) are a different story. In grizzly country, food storage is more complicated and crucial. Use freeze-dried food, which has minimal odor. If possible, do not sleep in the same clothes that you cooked and ate in; hang them with your food. Put all food and garbage in sealed plastic bags before loading and hanging stuff sacks. Sleep upwind from your kitchen area, and hang sacks so food odors do not waft over you.

Rangers at griz-country parks don't advocate counterbalancing. Since adult grizzlies cannot climb trees—although grizzly cubs can—they advise suspending food between two trees, 10 feet from the ground and four feet from each tree. Check with the National Park Service before venturing into grizzly backcountry for details on dealing with these unpredictable bruins.

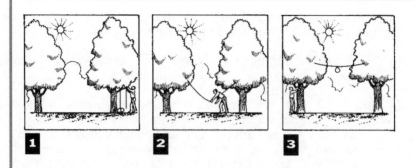

## CONVENTIONAL BEAR BAGGING

1) Find two trees about 20 feet apart. Throw weighted end of rope (about 100 feet long, at least ⅛-inch or larger nylon) over limb about 17 feet up. Tie off rope at base of tree.

2) Toss weighted end of rope over equally high branch of second tree. Affix food bag to midpoint of line with tied loop.

3) Hoist the bag, and tie off line to base of second tree. The bag must hang at least 12 feet from the ground.

Bears can figure out that chewing through your line gets them the goodies. A way to foil this practice—at least to buy yourself more time—is to use two lines rather than one, so when the bear chews through one line, your pack or food is still suspended.

## BEAR-BAGGING KIT

The biggest hassle when bear-bagging your food is getting the rope over the branch. As repeated tosses fall short of the mark or get tangled in the foliage, patience runs thin. Here's a way to improve both your aim and your temper.

Make a small (four by five inches or so) bag of rip-stop nylon, and add a grommet to each side of the bag near the top. The bag will hold 60 feet of $\frac{3}{32}$-inch nylon cord. When ready to bear-bag the food, put a rock in the bag and run the cord through the grommets, tying it with a bowline knot. Swing the bag around a couple times and loft it over the limb. Chances are it will improve your aim.

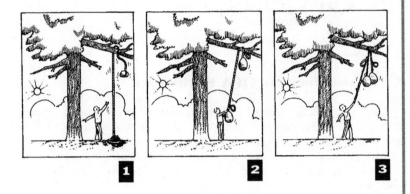

## COUNTERBALANCE BAGGING

1) Find a tree with a live, down-sloping branch at least 20 feet high, projecting at least 10 feet from the trunk. Toss weighted end of rope over section strong enough to hold the sacks but not the bear—about an inch in diameter.

2) Each sack should be of equal weight, ideally no more than 10 pounds each. Tie first sack to rope along with a retrieval loop. Pull it up. Tie second sack on as high as possible, and add another loop. Put excess rope in bag.

3) Toss second sack up so the pair balances evenly, at least 12 feet off ground, 10 feet from trunk, five feet below branch. Hook either loop with a stick to retrieve the bags.

*chapter four:*

# CONTROLLED BURN— YOUR FOOD-HEATING OPTIONS

## Care And Feeding Of A Pack Stove

An entire book could be written on the esoterica of camping stoves—the various designs, different fuels, and all the attendant strengths and weaknesses of the dozens of stoves on the market today. There are, however, some basic techniques that apply to stove safety and operation, regardless of the brand.

• Before you take a new stove on the trail, give it a few test runs at home. Carefully follow the manufacturer's directions. If you have questions, call a backpacking shop or the manufacturer.

• Pack stove and fuel in a side pocket, padded bag, or special stove case away from food and clothing. Don't nest the stove in a cook pot unless you like gas-flavored pilaf.

• Cook outside your tent. If you must cook inside, be sure to open the tent flap slightly even if the shelter has a vent, which should be open as well. With a flow of fresh air, you eliminate most danger of carbon monoxide poisoning and asphyxiation. If your tent cannot be adequately ventilated, do not cook inside.

• Use a stove base when cooking on snow, uneven ground, or a tent floor. A plywood scrap, ceramic tile, or an old license plate will do.

• The best stove won't work if you're out of fuel, so carry extra. Don't overfill the stove with fuel. Three-quarters full is better than too full. When a tank is too full, it can build up too much pressure while the stove is burning.

• Before filling a gas or kerosene stove, check the fuel for water or sediment. Bulk fuel sometimes develops condensation when stored. Use a filter funnel to keep debris from clogging your unit.

• Don't overprime, especially if you use your stove inside your tent. Excessive priming can cause a flare-up. One way to avoid too much fuel when priming is to use an eye dropper. The plastic kind won't break as easily as glass. If you should overprime your stove, sop up excess gas with a rag or tissue and lay it out on the ground a good distance away so the fuel can evaporate. Some people carry a squirt bottle of alcohol to use for priming. It causes less flare-up than gas.

• Replace the stove's fuel cap before priming.

• Keep the fuel-regulating valve closed while you prime the stove.

• If you spill fuel on a stove while filling it, clean the stove with a rag or tissue. Let the stove sit until excess fuel has evaporated before you light it. If fuel spills on the ground, move the stove to a new position. In a tent, spilled fuel should be cleaned up immediately and the tent aired adequately before you light your stove.

• Use the correct fuel. Multifuel stoves are a great option for globe-trotting packers but typically come with hefty price tags.

• Don't use oversize pots. A large pot will make the stove top-heavy, and it can be easily upset. On some stoves, a large pot will reflect heat back on the fuel tank and cause it to overheat.

• Avoid overheating the fuel tank. Feel the fuel tank occasionally. On gas stoves, tanks must be warm to generate pressure. On propane and butane stoves, cartridges should be cool to the touch. But if either a fuel tank or a cartridge feels hot, turn off the stove. Be sure it has cooled before you relight. On stoves where a flexible tube connects the burner to the fuel canister, keep both tubes and the fuel cartridges away from the burner.

• In wind, ensure that the stove's flame is blowing away from the fuel tank. Despite heat shields on some stoves, a flame blowing in the direction of the tank can overheat it.

• To increase efficiency, always cover pots and use wind-screens. Full wraparound windscreens are the most effective, though you must be careful not to enclose the fuel tank so tightly that the tank overheats. Blackened pots heat up faster than silvery new ones. Heat exchangers decrease boil times and fuel consumption.

• Turn the stove off if it is not working properly. Remove the pot, then check the stove thoroughly to make sure all connections are secure and the fuel tank is not overheating. Relight it. If the problem persists, eat cold food.

• Always carry stove-cleaning needles and spare parts. Maintenance is simple, but learn to make repairs before they're necessary.

• Refuel away from open flame.

• Turn off the stove before you check the fuel level or the cartridge connection.

• Do not refuel a hot stove. Sometimes a stove will run out of fuel in the middle of your cooking. Patience! Let the burner cool before you refuel. Not only is there a risk of the stove catching fire, but the fuel bottle can also go up in flames.

• Replace gas canisters with care. If the cartridge is difficult to screw in, don't force it because you could damage the valve. Before you start the stove, be sure the connection is secure. If you hear a faint hiss when you attach a new cartridge to a propane or butane stove, it may be leaking gas. Check the connection immediately. Try to solve the problem by attaching the cartridge properly. If gas continues to leak, replace the cartridge. One way to check for a leak is to touch the canister. Even a pin puncture on a butane cartridge will cause it to feel frosty. Also, avoid shaking gas canisters because the agitation could cause them to shoot up a large flame at start-up.

• Be sure caps on spare fuel bottles are replaced firmly after refueling. Always place the bottles several feet from your stove before you light it.

• Before you throw a cartridge away, make sure it is empty. If it still has fuel in it, light the stove and burn out the remaining fuel. Of course, pack the cartridge out with you.

• Clean your stove according to manufacturer's directions and as often as recommended. As fuel burns in a stove, it leaves a residue on the stove's innards. With use, this builds up. Trail grime and cooking spills can also clog parts. The buildup can cause your stove to burn unevenly.

• Treat your stove with care because it's delicate. If you should drop yours, check it out before you use it. Bent connections on fuel regulating valves can leak.

• If something goes wrong, think before you act. A moderate flare-up can get out of hand if you panic.

## How Altitude Affects Your Stove

As air density decreases with increasing height, the amount of oxygen available for combustion also decreases. The higher you backpack, the greater the decrease in available oxygen.

At 5,000 feet of elevation, air density is 86 percent of that at sea level. At 10,000 feet, it drops to 74 percent; at 14,000 feet, it falls to 65 percent; and at 20,320 feet (the summit of Mt. McKinley) it's 52 percent. Your lungs know this well. So does your stove because it too gets oxygen starved.

A stove must be able to take in enough oxygen to burn the fuel vapors it releases. Failing this, the stove runs too rich (as a car does), wastes fuel, and burns with a cooler, yellow-tipped flame.

If you're planning on spending a lot of time at altitude, shop for a stove accordingly. Some models have adjusting rings that allow for variations in air intake as necessary.

Decreased air density means less air pressure. As a result, water boils at a lower temperature at high elevations. At 5,200 feet, water boils at 201° F; at 9,000 feet, 196° F; and at 14,000 feet, 187° F. This gives the illusion of increased efficiency, but actually the opposite occurs. While a stove must spend less energy bringing water to boil at such heights, the lowered boiling point also means less efficient cooking. A three-minute egg boiled at sea level becomes a four-and-a-half-minute egg at 5,200 feet and a six-minute egg at 9,500 feet.

### A HIGH-COUNTRY OVEN YOU CAN MAKE AT HOME

Stoves have limitations, but with a few simple, lightweight, inexpensive additions, you can even bake a cake on the trail.

You'll need an unfluted aluminum gelatin-ring mold and two eight-inch aluminum-foil pie pans. The high-country oven consists of three parts:

1) the bottom heat spreader (one pie pan)

2) the ring mold (holds the batter)

3) the oven lid (the second pie pan)

The lid and ring mold are identical for all stoves. The bottom heat spreader might need slight modifications to fit securely on your particular stove.

To make the oven lid, cut two windows one inch high by two inches wide opposite each other on the side of the pie pan (A). These windows serve as vents for heat and steam to escape and as ports for viewing baking progress without removing the lid. The pie-pan lid fits upside down on top of the ring mold. No modification is needed for the mold.

The size and shape of the cutout in the center of the heat spreader depends on the kind of backpacking stove you own. To make the heat spreader, first measure the diameter of your stove's burner plate. Using a felt-tip marker, draw a circle the same size on the bottom of an aluminum-foil pie pan (B).

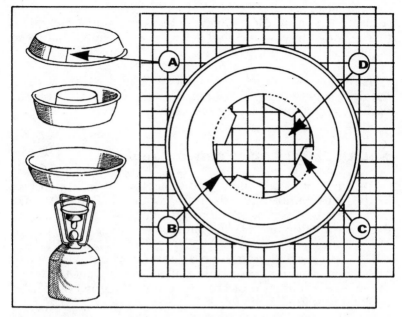

**Make a high-country oven out of a gelatin ring mold and two aluminum pie pans**

Now draw the anchor tabs, which hold the spreader securely to the stove along the inside of the circle perimeter (C).

Three or four equally spaced tabs should do; you may have to experiment to determine the proper number and location of tabs for your particular stove. Each tab is two inches wide at the base and extends 1 1/2 inches into the circle, the sides forming lines that intersect in the center of the circle. Put the pie tin on a flat, firm surface. With a hobby knife or single-edge razor blade, cut out the circle and tab combination that fits your stove (D). Test the heat spreader for a stable, secure fit. Here again, you'll have to fiddle around to determine how to best attach the heat spreader to your stove.

A heavier, more durable and sturdier heat spreader can be made from an aluminum or steel pie pan. A pair of tin snips will be needed to cut out the pattern.

Your high-country oven is now ready. For camp purposes,

the easiest mixes are the best, at least until you get the hang of using the oven. Most supermarkets carry numerous mixes that require only water, and refrigerated doughs that need nothing added and stay fresh for days if wrapped in foil.

Using a low to medium flame, the high-country oven requires slightly longer baking time than indicated on the package directions. Bring on the cake!

### Not All Flames Are Created Equal

For environmental, safety, and aesthetic reasons, open fires in the backcountry are usually discouraged. Portable back-packing stoves are light, more efficient, and vastly simpler than constructing fire pits and gathering wood.

Yet you may find yourself in a situation where you want to or have to cook on an open fire. If so, you'll want to choose the most efficient style of fire for your cooking needs. Not all cooking fires are equal.

The purpose of a cooking fire is twofold: to contain the fire, and to hold cooking utensils and food in a precise and easily adjusted relationship to the heat source.

Think of a camp cooking fireplace as a kitchen stove with peculiar adjustments. On the stove, you increase or decrease the heat by adjusting the fuel flow. On the open campfire, fuel supply is a fairly coarse adjustment, so the distance between heat source and food becomes the fine adjustment. Human ingenuity has given us several options here.

**The hunter fire:** This type has a single pole over the flame, from which the pots hang. Generally, the pots are too high, requiring far too much wood and time to get the cooking done. But this fire does fit the traditional image of a camp kitchen.

**The dingle crane, or stick, fire:** This slightly less compli-cated cooking arrangement is a pole stuck, wedged, or propped at an angle to hold a pot over the fire. It works best if the food is actually on the spit, as with shish kabobs or twists (biscuit dough twisted around the stick and baked).

**Hunter Fire**                    **Dingle Crane Fire**

Often, too, some food can be buried in the coals and cooked. Wrap the food in aluminum foil, cover with a half inch of clay, then surround with hot coals.

You can reduce the impact of this or any kind of campfire by building it on a **flat rock** covered with several inches of soil. The soil should cover an area slightly larger than the fire. Burn all wood completely. After the fire is out, crush and scatter the coals, remove the soil, and rinse the surface of the rock.

**Trapper and trench fireplaces:** These are the most common type of camp fireplaces if you don't count those awful three-blocks-and-a-grate monstrosities in established campgrounds. The trapper is an almost-parallel row of rocks, tapering together slightly at the down-wind end, with the fire between them. The pots rest on these rows and the fire is fed from the ends.

**Flat-Rock Fire**                **Trapper Fireplace**

The trench is simply the trapper fire turned inside-out with the space for the fire hollowed out of the ground and the pots resting on the edge of the undisturbed soil. The windward end of the trench should slope gently to the bottom to let air in to feed the fire.

If you are ever forced to dig out a pit for a fire, such as in a survival situation, carefully remove sod or topsoil in large chunks. Set these to one side in a neat pile, then remove underlying soil to form your pit. Pile the bare soil around the edge of the pit to keep the fire from drying out nearby vegetation. Before you break camp the next morning, both the sides and bottom of the pit must be cool. Remaining coals should be crushed to a fine powder. Cover the coals with the bare soil and carefully replace the topsoil or sod. Make sure the chunks fit neatly and snugly. Finally, scatter leaves, twigs, rocks, or duff over the area to create a natural appearance.

**Tripod fireplace:** With a tripod fireplace, a single pot can be balanced on three rocks or even on metal tent pegs. The fire (or better yet, coals) is situated between the legs of the tripod. It's big enough for only one pot.

**Reflector fireplace:** The reflector fireplace is a near-vertical wall of logs, sod, aluminum foil, or rock that reflects the radiant heat of the fire into a reflector oven. The smoother the reflector, the better it works. Plastering the reflector with mud often helps, especially with a log reflector, since it also helps fireproof it. Aluminum foil is probably the most efficient material. The flames must reach the top of the reflector for maximum effectiveness, so it is a fire system reserved for areas with plenty of available down wood.

**Trench Fireplace**          **Tripod Fireplace**

**Reflector Fireplace**                    **Keyhole Fire**

**Keyhole fire:** Most cooking is easier when done over coals instead of flames, the reflector fire being the exception. Coal fires keep pots cleaner, have more even heat distribution, and are easily regulated by adding and subtracting coals, which minimizes lifting the utensils. The keyhole fire is basically a coal factory.

The rectangular part of the keyhole shape is the inside of a trapper or trench-type fireplace. The round part holds a normal tepee fire that's allowed to burn down to coals, which are then scraped into the standard fireplace. If there is a lot of cooking to do, two tepee fires can be alternated so one is burning while the other is being rebuilt or scraped away.

The flame part of the keyhole can be used with a reflector and reflector oven. This gets in the way of coal transfer somewhat, but it can be managed if you are careful.

**Altar, or raised-platform, fireplace:** Almost any type of fireplace (except perhaps those requiring the digging of holes) can be placed on an altar or raised platform. The altar fireplace is made of logs or rocks, and fireproofed with dirt. The fire is built on top of that. A reflector keyhole on an altar fireplace is about as close to a kitchen stove as you can get in the woods. However, except for base camps and other semi-permanent establishments, it just takes too long to build.

**Omaha, or Dakota, fireplace:** The Omaha, or Dakota fireplace is ideal for prairies and other areas of high wind. It consists of two holes in the ground about six inches apart and a foot to a foot-and-a-half deep. A tunnel about two inches in

| **Altar Fireplace** | **Omaha Fireplace** |

diameter connects these holes at the bottom. A fire is built in one hole and a pot is placed over the hole, covering it completely. The other hole furnishes the air for the fire, and the smoke (what little there is) escapes around the pot. A tablespoon is the traditional tool for digging the fireplace.

**Banked fire:** When matches are running low, a fire can be kept alive overnight by banking it. Let it burn into a large log so plenty of coals are produced. Cover the coals with ashes and then dry dirt or sand, putting out the flames but not smothering the coals. Cover the whole mound with a tarp or something waterproof in case of rain. The next morning, dig out the glowing coals and start your fire.

*chapter five:*
# ADDING LIFE
# TO A BLAND MENU

## Spice It Up

There's a long-held backpacking notion that anything cooked in the woods tastes great. Proponents of said theory hold that after tasting trail dust all day and washing it down with iodine-flavored water, even tree bark is savory.

As with most long-held notions, this is not absolutely true. Truth be told, much of what we Backwoods Betty Crockers conjure is less than lip smacking. Some of it is downright tasteless. But being on the trail doesn't mean you have to leave your taste buds at home. To rescue bland and tasteless backcountry meals, you merely need a bit of imagination, a few basic spices from home, and a willingness to try something new.

Want to add Italian flair to your tomato-based dinner? Add dried basil and oregano, which can be mixed and carried in the same container. Lend an Indian flavor to your chicken and rice (or any bland chicken dish) by tossing in some curry and a few raisins from your gorp. Even a rich dish can benefit from curry and raisins. Cumin will make a bean dish more "Mexican."

Two seasonings you shouldn't leave home without are garlic powder and onion powder. Don't be timid with the onion powder because it can enhance nearly every meal. Go lighter on the garlic, though, unless you're exceptionally fond of it and want to hike alone. (If you're trying to limit salt intake for health reasons, avoid garlic and onion salts.) Dehydrated garlic and onion flakes supply even more flavor but must be added while you're cooking so they can rehydrate. Dried parsley lacks a strong flavor and isn't worth the space it takes up in your pack. Cinnamon and nutmeg are easy to carry and can make bland oatmeal more palatable. Banana chips, chopped dates, raisins, and other dried fruits are also easy additions to oatmeal.

Bouillon is another good flavor enhancer for chicken or beef dishes but often contains extra salt. Individually wrapped bouillon cubes stay moisture-free longer than granules, which tend to clump and harden. Borvil, a dark, sweet-smelling liquid, has a delicious beefy taste and can be used in place of bouillon. It's found in larger, well-stocked grocery stores or gourmet shops.

Bouillon cubes should be carried in their own small, sealed plastic bag since they melt in the heat. Package all powders, herbs and spices at home in individual plastic bags, enclosing directions for mixing if necessary.

For more basic food rescue, add instant tomato or cheddar powder. Grated Parmesan and Romano cheeses also travel well. Instant soups like cream of mushroom and cream of chicken are also good flavorers, and come in easy-to-carry envelopes. Dried butter-flavored bits usually found in the spice section of the grocery store, squeezable margarine, or a stick of margarine kept in a wide-mouth water bottle are light-weight flavor enhancers. The extra fat is essential on a long trip when body fat reserves are used up.

Don't neglect other seasonings that might seem exotic. Dried mushrooms, bacon bits, flavored croutons, and sesame, poppy, and sunflower seeds are all easy to pack and light-weight.

So now that you've got flavor, does your meal still have the consistency of gruel? Watery stews aren't nearly as filling and hearty as those with thick gravy. If you've already added spices, use milk, tomato, and cheese powders to thicken things up. Or you can make gravy by simply adding a small amount of flour to a little cold water in your cup, stirring until the flour dissolves and adding it to your stew. One-and-a-half tablespoons of flour will effectively thicken one cup of liquid. A little cornstarch or arrowroot powder works just as well.

If you choose, you can take along packets of commercial gravy mixes found in the grocery store. Merely follow the directions on the envelope, and add water to the dry mix little by little. Dump the envelope's contents into a pot of water or soup and you'll end up with undissolved gravy chunks that will raise the hair on the back of your neck when you bite into one.

If you want to avoid the additives in commercial gravy and sauce mixes, either make your own, or carry instant potato flakes or instant baby cereal in a sealed plastic bag. The tiny freeze-dried crystals thicken and bulk up your meal in seconds and can be added to the pot without premixing. Baby cereals are a wonderful source of additive-free grains, and come in a variety of choices that add bulk and protein. If you're feeling adventurous, mix up your own white sauce at home. Add one tablespoon of dried butter morsels, one-and-a half tablespoons flour, and two tablespoons of powdered milk. Label and put in a bag with the directions, "Add one cup of water." It makes a medium-thick sauce to serve three.

You might be tempted to stretch your prepackaged meals by adding a package of Ramen noodles to something like a prefab Lipton Noodle Dinner to "make it go further." The result is always a lot of noodles and little, if any, taste. What you should do instead is increase the seasonings along with the bulk. If someone runs out of food and you have to stretch a prepackaged dinner, look at the package, see what herbs and spices the manufacturer added, then add more of the same seasonings. If it's a creamy dish, add instant milk and some water. Always pack more instant milk than you'll need for cereal and instant puddings; besides making a dish creamier, milk adds protein and calcium.

Garlic bread is an easy-to-make side dish for any meal, but is especially nice if you're eating Italian. First, melt a little margarine in a pan, sprinkle garlic powder and Italian spices on a slice of buttered bread, then lightly fry on both sides. To make a Danish for breakfast, fry bread the same way, then add cinnamon and brown sugar.

One more suggestion: If all else fails, cayenne (red) pepper can be used as a last resort. It won't give you much variety, but you can rest assured your dinner won't be bland.

## Grow A Garden In Your Pack

You're going backpacking. No fresh fruits, no vegetables, no greens. Not quite.

You can grow a garden of sprouts in your backpack. Gastronomically speaking, sprouts can be a boon to backcountry cuisine. These just-add-water foods offer everything you want backpacking food to be: lightweight, tasty, nutritious, easy to prepare, and packaged in durable, compact, and biodegradable containers (seeds).

Sprouts can bolster a flagging appetite because they come in a variety of flavors ranging from the pleasant, nutlike crunch of mung beans to the spicy accent of radishes. They can be eaten raw as a salad or added to anything from scrambled eggs to chili. For the trail-weary palate, particularly on trips of a week or more, their vegetable-like freshness is a welcome respite from reconstituted foods. Even for weekend outings, these easy-to-store and simple-to-prepare greens make an excellent addition to the food bag. Just be sure to get a batch started a few days before you leave home.

Sprouting seeds on the trail is easy; a little water and a few rinses, and nature does the rest. Seeds were once available only at specialty health-food stores but can now be found at supermarkets. Because many garden seeds have been chemically treated and are unfit for consumption, be sure to purchase seeds that are intended for sprouting. The only other items you'll need are a wide-mouthed plastic quart water bottle, a mesh lid or piece of cheesecloth, and several rubber bands.

Soak the seeds in water for eight to 12 hours. Not surprisingly, small seeds like alfalfa require the least soaking time, and big seeds like mung beans require the most. To avoid contamination with Giardia or other waterborne organisms, always use filtered or chemically treated water. If possible, leave the bottle in the sun to warm the water before adding seeds. This speeds germination. Mix at a ratio of about four parts water to one part seeds.

After soaking, drain the seeds through the mesh lid or the

piece of cheesecloth secured over the bottle's mouth with the rubber bands. If it's near mealtime, save the water for a stock. Pour the seeds into a cup and place a small piece of clean cloth or paper towel in the bottom of the bottle (the side of the bottle if it will be resting sideways in your pack). Put the seeds back in the bottle and replace the rubber-band-held cheesecloth or mesh lid. Store the bottle in your pack wrapped in layers of clothing to keep it insulated from temperature extremes and away from the sun.

Sprouts should be rinsed at least twice a day, and some seeds produce the best results when rinsed three or four times daily. Simply remove the paper towel or cloth, add enough water to cover the sprouts, and gently swirl the bottle. Drain the water and return the towel after wringing it somewhat dry; keep the seeds moist but not wet. Replace the lid. Most sprouts can be harvested (eaten!) in three to five days. Don't leave them too long, though, because they'll develop a bitter taste.

Don't hesitate to experiment. Add Parmesan cheese to a mix of sprouts with a spicy vinaigrette. Use alfalfa sprouts in place of lettuce. Make a slaw out of mung beans, sunflower, and radish sprouts. Add them to pancakes and stews, or just eat them while you walk.

### *Alfalfa seeds:*
Yield: 3 Tbsp. seeds = 4 cups sprouts
Rinses per day: two
Sprouting time: three to five days. Grow well with mung beans.
Flavor: mild. Replacement for lettuce. Can be exposed to sun (if kept from overheating) to green before eating.

### *Amaranth seeds:*
Yield: 3 Tbsp. seeds = 1 cup sprouts
Rinses per day: three
Sprouting time: two to three days
Flavor: mild. A popular food of the Aztecs, it was suppressed by conquistadors because of its association with rituals of human sacrifice. The seeds are about the size of mustard seeds, with a protein content 16 percent higher than wheat or corn.

**Mung beans:**
  Yield: 1 cup = 4 to 5 cups
  Rinses per day: three to five
  Sprouting time: three to five days. Easy to sprout.
  Flavor: crunchy and nutlike. Great in stir-fry.

**Mustard seeds:**
  Yield: 2 tablespoons = 3 cups
  Rinses per day: two
  Sprouting time: three to five days
  Flavor: spicy and tangy like fresh mustard. A versatile flavoring for salads and cooked dishes.

**Peas:**
  Yield: 1 cup = 1½ cups
  Rinses per day: two to three
  Sprouting time: three days
  Flavor: like fresh peas. Excellent trail munchie. Great in salads or as a vegetable side dish with dinner.

**Radish seeds:**
  Yield: 1 tablespoon = 1 cup.
  Rinses per day: two
  Sprouting time: two to six days
  Flavor: hot and tangy. Good addition to salads.

**Sesame seeds (unhulled):**
  Yield: ½ cup = 1½ cups
  Rinses per day: four
  Sprouting time: three days
  Flavor: rich sesame flavor. Great in salads and stir-fry. Bitter if grown more than $1/16$ inch.

**Sunflower seeds:**
  Yield: ½ cup = 1½ cups
  Rinses per day: two
  Sprouting time: one to three days
  Flavor: nutty. Another excellent trail munchie. Great in salads or as an addition to spaghetti sauce or chili.

**Wheat:**
  Yield: 1 cup = 3 ½ to 4 cups
  Rinses per day: two to three
  Sprouting time: two to four days

Flavor: sweet and nutty. Easy to sprout. Try in salads and pancakes.

### ONE WILD PLANT YOU KNOW AND WON'T FORGET

Foraging for edible wild plants can help you expand your trail diet. Proper plant identification generally requires a good field guide and some experience—there are dangerous plants out there! But there's one edible plant probably nobody would miss—the common dandelion.

The dandelion plant is totally edible. The spicy leaves are most often eaten either in salads or boiled as greens, but the roots and flowers should not be ignored. Try these two root recipes next time you find yourself in a field of dandelions:

### *Boiled Roots With Butter*

Wash the roots and remove all root hairs. Boil for 20 minutes until hot but not mushy. Drain, and add butter, salt, and pepper to taste.

### *Dandelion Coffee*

Wash several roots in warm water. Dry in a moderate oven for two hours or until the roots are brittle and dark brown. Allow the roots to cool, then grind them to powder. For each cup of boiling water, add one teaspoon of root powder and let steep 15 minutes.

## Hold The Salt

Many people feel that an open coastline, where elements merge under salty spray, is food for the soul. However, few take time to nourish their physical being with what the coasts offer. Depending on the time of year, you can gather wild food on nearly any seacoast in North America, from Florida to Nova Scotia, from Mexico to Alaska, even the Arctic.

But before you head down to the shore with knife and fork in hand, follow a few rules of the field, which hold true for foraging inland as well. Always refer to dependable regional field guides, which help you identify edible plants or shellfish and give information about the range and frequency of a species and other interesting lore.

Never eat any plant or animal you cannot identify or that you are not absolutely positive is safe to eat! If shellfishing, listen to reports broadcast daily by the National Oceanic and Atmospheric Administration on weather-band radio that give locations closed by "red tide," an infestation of microorganisms that makes shellfish poisonous during warm months.

In all foraging, consider the impact you have on the environment. Don't disturb surrounding plant or animal life, and take only what you will use. Don't take anything if a plant or algae isn't abundant, and try to pick leaves or fronds without killing the plant.

## NORTH ATLANTIC

A trailing green plant with purple flowers on one- to two-inch pods, **beach peas** look like a smaller version of common garden peas. Although the peas are somewhat undersized, and it takes some time to shuck enough from their pods for a meal, they taste much like garden peas and can be used in the same way. Look for beach peas behind ridges of beach grass or around flotsam left by storms on sand beaches from New Jersey to Labrador. It's best to pick in August when the pods ripen. For those less inclined to shucking, try frying the tender pods whole in butter, then add to scalloped potatoes for a marvelous beachside entree.

**Scotch lovage,** a parsleylike herbaceous plant that grows up to two feet with glossy, dark-green leaves, is also called sea lovage or wild beach celery. The leaves have a pungent taste not unlike parsley or celery leaves. Scotch lovage grows in gravelly and sandy coastal soils, typically among beach grasses or along the edges of salt marshes. It is found from New England to Nova Scotia and also in Alaska, where coastal natives have used it for centuries. The stems and leaves are best picked before the plant is mantled with pinkish-white blossoms in early July, though tender leaves may be picked from fully grown plants all summer long, especially the young ones that sprout regularly (like parsley leaves) between the maturing stems.

Snipped into shreds, Scotch lovage makes an excellent companion to seafood. Heap generously over butter-fried mussels or fish as they poach. Or simply steam gently with a little water in a pan over a slow fire and eat as a cooked vegetable. Nibbled fresh, Scotch lovage offers a healthy dose of vitamins A and C.

Along the high-tide mark on sand beaches in Maine, you should notice **sea blite** along with **orach,** a vinelike herb with two-inch arrowhead-shaped leaves, growing strictly in salt-rich sand. Both orach and sea blite are relatives of spinach and can be prepared similarly. They are naturally salt-flavored and the leaves make wonderful raw greens for a salad. When boiled, they become tasty vegetable greens. The best time to pick orach is in July because it is more tender before it blooms. Orach is superb with scrambled eggs. Simply fry a few chopped leaves in butter until tender, and add eggs. Sprinkle with cheese if you like.

**Irish moss** is a frilly marine algae three to six inches high with flat, progressively forking fronds, often found in unbroken mats in shallow tidepools. Its color ranges from green to ochre to purplish brown. You have probably eaten Irish moss because it contains large amounts of carrageenan, a substance used in making ice cream, gelatin, even beer. In Maine, "mossers" harvested the plant for commercial use. The Irish have gathered and eaten the moss for more than 600 years, hence the name.

While Irish moss has a supple, leathery texture when freshly picked (easily done by wading along the low-tide mark and gently pulling the plants free), boiling transforms it into a gelatinous "pudding" with a delicate sea flavor. Top with a bit of vanilla, milk, and sugar for a treat New Englanders have enjoyed for years. Irish moss is spiny and tough when dried, but easily reconstituted by boiling 30 to 40 minutes.

For their food value and availability up and down the Atlantic coast, shellfish can't be beat. Look for **mussels** clinging to rocks, ledges, or on the surface of sand and gravel bars just below half-tide line. **Steamer clams** grow three to six inches down in mud or gravel bottoms. Spot their breather holes in the sand below half-tide line, and unearth them with your hands or a clam rake.

## SOUTH ATLANTIC

Perhaps the most ubiquitous seaside edible is **glasswort,** or **saltwort,** found on sand beaches and in salt marshes along both coasts of North America but especially near dry-grass upland marshes from the mid-Atlantic states south. Glasswort is a low succulent plant six to eight inches high with branching, jointed tendrils filled with salty sap. It is typically green, but an orange-red variety can be found in some marshes.

Because of its texture and the shape of its tendrils, glasswort is sometimes called "beach asparagus." Coastal residents commonly pickle glasswort, likening the flavor to watermelon rind. But coastal foragers can enjoy it either on its own or in a salad after boiling the tendrils for just a few minutes until tender. Glasswort is best picked in July before it gets tough.

**Sea rocket** is an abundant, easily found wild herb good for flavoring seafoods and salads. It is a low, fleshy plant with succulent branching stems that taste like mild horseradish. Rocket-shaped seed pods form shortly after a late-summer bloom of dainty lavender flowers.

You'll find sea rocket along high-tide marks on sand beaches, sometimes following the scalloped patterns of waves where seeds have washed up and germinated on shore. Its fleshy root, when dried and ground, has been used in bread-making as an additive to flour. As a forager, you'll find the leaves and stems of early summer most useful. Chopped and cooked with other vegetables and seafood, or added raw to wild or domestic salads, it adds a delightful tang.

You will typically find **oysters** exposed at low tide on cord-grass silt banks or in nutrient-rich shallow water along the tidal marsh areas of Virginia, the Carolinas, and Georgia. No oyster tongs or diving required. Oysters, clams, and other shellfish find the rich nutrients of the marsh especially nice for breeding, and they can be had in plenty.

While some people prefer to eat oysters raw, it takes a little ingenuity to get a live one open. Insert a blunt, sharp knife into the clamped edge of the oyster and manipulate it side to side to cut the strong muscles holding the shell halves together. It helps to knock off a bit of the edge to expose part of the muscle to the knife. Gloves are recommended to prevent cuts from the sharp shell. Once open, simply trim out the meat and enjoy the hard-earned delicacy. Steaming over a few cups of boiling water or grilling over a slow fire will open oysters more readily. Cooked oysters are especially good dipped in melted butter laced with lemon juice and shredded sea rocket.

## WEST COAST

**Hottentot fig** is a succulent, mat-forming plant with long, trailing stems bearing yellow daisylike flowers that turn pink with age. By July the flowers start forming a fleshy, figlike brown fruit that makes a wonderful campfire jam. The Hottentot fig festoons coastal sands and bluffs from Mexico to southern Oregon, where it was introduced from South Africa to stabilize dunes. The tongue-twisting genus name, *Mesembryanthemum* (blooming at midday) is a useful identification clue. Chop up a handful of the plump fruits and boil in a cup of water, then add a cup or two of sugar and stir until syrupy. Spoon liberally over campfire toast, hot cereal or beach-strawberry pancakes.

Yes, **beach strawberry**. It's a common perennial coastal herb that grows up to eight inches high, with trifoliate-toothed leaves and red berries that ripen through midsummer. It's easily found underfoot on dunes and bluffs from Alaska to South America, where its Chilean relative was used for developing hybrid domestic strains of strawberries. Look for its distinctive five-petaled white blossoms, which bloom simultaneously with the ripening fruit. Eat the berries raw, cooked as jam, or mixed with bread and pancake batters. Both the berries and the leaves, which make a decent tea, are high in vitamin C.

**Dulse** is a seaweed that's edible when cooked or dried but not raw. It's a translucent purple-red algae with up to one-foot-long leafy, flat lobes and is usually found clustered on rocky shores exposed during low tide. It is common along subarctic intertidal zones of both the Pacific and Atlantic coasts and in sheltered lagoons away from surging seas. A delicate plant, it's easy to pull from the rocks by hand. Asians as well as Alaskan natives cook dulse with soups and chowders. It is rubbery eaten raw, but takes on a pleasing texture after drying in the sun. Dulse, like many seaweeds, provides a healthy natural source of iodine.

Edible **kelp** should not be underestimated as a good sea-side edible. You'll find kelp in the surging shallows during low tide, usually growing in thick beds anchored in rocky bottoms. It ranges from California, Washington, and Oregon to Hawaii and Japan. It's also found on the Atlantic coast. Edible kelp has a characteristically long and wavy central frond about six inches wide, growing from one to 10 feet high from a short basal stem where a number of shorter fronds grow radially outward. It is olive green or brown and is frequently found floating freely in the water, but a little wading and tugging will invariably reveal lots to eat. Kelp makes a nutritious additive to chowders, soups, and stews, and adds punch to any trail casserole.

**Butter clams** are another low-tide delicacy sometimes available to the western beachcomber. Clams, in general, prefer shallow-water gravel where they can burrow from predators yet find a steady supply of waterborne, siphonable nutrients. At low tide, a few exposed shells usually give away a clam bed. But often, a tiny jet of water shooting from the sand under a footfall betrays their presence; then you dig. You'll need a shovel or clam rake. Explore an area a few inches deep. Don't excavate an entire clam bed to exhaustion. While more plentiful along the California coast, butter clams may also be harvested on Mexican, Washington, and Oregon beaches. Unlike oysters, clams are easy to pry open with a knife. But steaming works well for almost any shellfish.

### Don't Slap That Bug! Eat It!

Inhaling a gnat or accidentally swallowing a fly is probably most people's only experience with ingesting insects. Yet bugs have long been a staple in diets of people throughout time and around the world.

Insects were popular fare among the Aztecs; several bug species were treasured by the elite. Today, in Mexico more than 200 insect species are used as food. To the north, in the arid region of the United States that we know as the Great Basin, Native Americans once dined on a menu of insects that included ants, beetles, caterpillars, grasshoppers, and fly larvae. In regions of Zaire, more than one-third of people's dietary protein comes from insects. Throughout Asia and the

Pacific, insects are highly prized. Japanese emperor Hirohito's favorite dish was rice with wasps. The Thais use ants as a condiment and the Koreans relish the pupae of the silkworm.

The United States, on the other hand, is one of the few places where insects aren't eaten. Our culinary snobbery likely has more to do with European cultural bias than a supposedly refined palate. Insects just don't look like what we've learned to consider as food, although there are several glaring exceptions among our most elegant dishes. Lobster is considered a highly desirable food, in spite of the fact that it belongs to the phylum *Arthropoda*, which also includes insects.

Vincent M. Holt, in his 1885 book *Why Not Eat Insects?*, asks how we can swallow "loathsome looking oysters . . . raw and living" for an appetizer, yet be repulsed by the presence of a caterpillar in boiled cabbage? Good question. Holt had high hopes that we might someday move past our aversion to eating insects. "It may require a strong effort of will to reason ourselves out of the stupid prejudices that have stood in our way for ages," he writes, "but what is the good of the advanced state of the times if we cannot thus cast aside these prejudices. . . ."

Little has changed in the century since Holt wrote those words, although the past few years have seen renewed interest in edible insects. Research into the potential of insects as human food and animal feed is being conducted at several United States universities, and the National Aeronautics and Space Administration has been examining insects as a food source for long-term space flight.

Much of the reason for renewed interest in edible insects is their sheer abundance. Grasshoppers are so common that hundreds of thousands of pounds have been gathered by Great Basin Indians with only a few days labor. Another Native American favorite, the caterpillars of the Pandora moth, are so prevalent that populations of the adult moth in the dry sparseness of the Arizona desert have been estimated at 100,000 per hectare—nearly one for each square foot. The moths were known to the Indians as Pe-ag-gah, the "good to eat" or "big fat ones."

It has been estimated that as much as 100 pounds of insect

protein per acre can be found in the Oregon countryside. In the tropics that number jumps to 400 pounds per acre. Insects constitute a sizeable crop of foragable food that could lighten the load of any backpack. Just look at it as a way to bite back.

## RECIPES

### *Tempura Grasshoppers*

Pluck wings and legs. Dip in batter and fry in oil until golden brown. Serve with soy sauce mixed with dry mustard.

### *Cicada Smorgasbord*

Newly hatched cicadas are best because their shells haven't hardened. With adults, pluck wings and legs. Place cicadas in pan and roast over heat for 10 to 15 minutes. When dry, grind coarsely, and sprinkle on food for a nutty taste. Or drop cicadas in boiling water, coat with red pepper, garlic, and ground bay leaf. Or stir fry with garlic, and add your freeze-dried meal packet.

*chapter six:*
# THE RECIPES

The following recipes were gathered from 20 years of reader input, and although BACKPACKER editors weren't able to personally field test all of them, we feel confident in recommending them to you. However, whether it's a stove, boots, or a recipe for lentil stew, it's always a good idea to try out anything new at home or over a weekend before heading into the backcountry for a longer trip. Who knows, you might even find a dish that's too good to reserve just for camping!

## How To Make Water Delicious

### *Make Your Own Coffee Bags*

For that morning cup of fresh ground coffee, make inexpensive coffee bags (like tea bags) out of drip coffee filters. At home, add a single-cup measure of ground coffee to a filter (A), cut the paper filter down to size (B), fold the top over (C), and sew it shut on a sewing machine or by hand (D). Knotting the loose threads at the end makes for easy retrieval when the coffee is done. In camp, simply toss a bag into your cup, add hot water, swirl and enjoy.

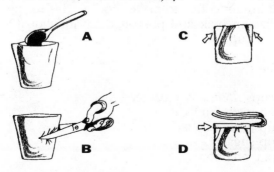

### Frothy Fruit Drink

This delicious drink can be prepared in minutes.
½ cup (1 packet) powdered fruit drink
½ cup powdered milk

Into your one-quart water bottle pour about a half-cup of water, then the dry ingredients. Slosh around a bit and fill the bottle about two-thirds full with water. Shake vigorously, then top it off with water and give a few more shakes. You can use cold water in the summer, which gives the drink the semblance of a milk shake, or in cold weather, use hot water.

### Hot Minted Chocolate

1 part unsweetened cocoa powder
1 part instant mint-tea powder
2 parts powdered milk
3 parts brown sugar

At home, mix ingredients and store in plastic bag. In camp, add two heaping tablespoons of mixture to a cup of hot water and stir until dissolved. When packing for the trail, allow one ounce of dry mixture per person per serving.

### Instant Hot Chocolate

1 box (8 qt.) powdered milk
2 lb. box Nestle's Quik
1 jar (10 to 12 oz.) non-dairy creamer

At home, mix ingredients and store in plastic bag. To serve, pour boiling water over one-quarter cup mixture and serve. If desired, add instant coffee to make mocha. This recipe can be mixed together in bulk and portioned for individual servings of one-quarter cup each.

### Mac's Coffee

1½ cups non-dairy creamer
⅓ cup malted milk
¼ cup instant coffee
½ cup sugar
1 tsp. cinnamon

At home, mix dry ingredients. Package in a plastic bottle or make individual packets in plastic bags. In camp, add three tablespoons of mixture to each cup and mix in boiling water.

### Palatable Powdered Milk

Powdered milk is an excellent source of much-needed protein in a backpacker's diet. But if the thought of mixing it with water and drinking it straight makes you sick, try spicing it up a bit this way:

> 1 cup powdered milk
> 3 cups water
> ½ Tbsp. cinnamon
> pinch of nutmeg
> honey to sweeten, if desired

Mix the milk and then scald it—don't boil it! Then mix the spices and add them to the milk. Stir well, sweeten to taste, and drink while warm.

### Spiced Tea

For a before-bed drink or as a warm-up after any chilling activity:

> 2 cups Tang
> ½ cup instant tea
> 1 pkg. (1 qt.) powdered lemonade
> 1½ cups sugar
> 1 tsp. cinnamon
> 1 tsp. ground cloves

At home, mix ingredients, and store in plastic bag. To serve, add about three spoonfuls of tea to a cup of boiling water and stir.

### Trail Shake

> ⅓ cup powdered milk
> 2 Tbsp. non-dairy creamer
> 1 Tbsp. custard mix
> 1 envelope Instant Breakfast, any flavor
> 1¼ cups cold water

At home, mix the powdered milk, creamer and custard, and store in plastic bag. On the trail, mix with Instant Breakfast and water. Place in a container with a tight-fitting lid and shake vigorously. For extra richness, add malt to taste.

## Breakfasts—Nutritious Ways To Start The Day

### Breakfast Booster

½ tsp. salt
2 oz. condensed mincemeat
1½ cups water
1½ cups quick-cooking rolled oats

Add salt and crumbled mincemeat to water, and bring to boil. Add rolled oats, stirring constantly, and cook for one minute or longer. Adding powdered milk to the mix will enhance its nutritional value and taste. Serves two. A nine-ounce package of mincemeat and an 18-ounce box of oats will provide nine servings.

### Breakfast Cake

⅔ cup sugar
3 Tbsp. powdered milk
1½ cups biscuit mix
½ cup packed brown sugar
¾ cup chopped nuts
¾ cup water
1 egg
2 Tbsp. butter

At home, mix sugar and powdered milk with biscuit mix, and store in plastic bag. Mix brown sugar and nuts in another plastic bag. In camp, mix water and egg with biscuit mixture to form batter. Pour into a greased pan and bake in reflector oven (or Dutch oven) about 20 minutes or until brown. Melt butter, mix with sugar and nuts, and spread on top of cake. Brown a few minutes and eat hot with butter.

## *Camp Cereal*

> 1 cup cracked wheat
> 1 cup quick-cooking rolled oats
> ¼ cup packed brown sugar
> ½ cup dried chopped apples (or other dried fruit)
> ½ cup raisins

At home, mix all ingredients and store in plastic bag. In camp, place mixture into cooking pot (amount will vary with your appetite). Add just enough water to cover top of cereal. Let stand overnight. By morning the raisins will have puffed up and look like grapes. Heat, adding enough water to keep the cereal from sticking, and stir occasionally.

## *Cornmeal Flappers*

> 1⅓ cups cornmeal
> ¼ cup powdered milk
> ⅔ cup flour
> 1 tsp. salt
> ¼ cup baking powder
> 1 Tbsp. oil
> 1 Tbsp. molasses
> 2 cups boiling water

At home, mix dry ingredients and store in plastic bag. In camp, add oil, and boiling water. Mix well. Cook in any size pan on a hot oiled griddle. When browned on bottom, turn once and cook on other side. Serve with stewed fruit, honey, or syrup. Serves three or four.

## *Cornmeal Mush*

Cornmeal mush is lightweight, nourishing, and versatile. Seasoned with salt, pepper, paprika, and grated Parmesan cheese, it becomes polenta, an excellent lunch or supper. With honey and wheat germ, it is a nourishing breakfast. It is unsurpassed as a dessert with chopped walnuts and your favorite jam. Or you can add cheese to the mush, or sauté slices of mush and pour maple syrup over them.

½ cup yellow cornmeal
⅔ cup powdered milk
2 Tbsp. soy flour (optional)
2 cups water
½ tsp. salt
1 or 2 eggs (optional)

At home mix dry ingredients and store in plastic bag. In camp, add a half cup water to make a smooth paste. Boil remaining water and paste slowly, stirring constantly until the mixture is thick. Remove from heat, then stir in eggs and whatever condiments you like. Serves two.

### Cream Of Wheat Feast

1 cup water
½ cup Cream of Wheat
⅓ cup shredded coconut
¼ tsp. maple extract or vanilla
¼ cup slivered almonds

Boil water. Add Cream of Wheat. Stir well, then add other ingredients. Serve hot, topped with brown sugar or honey and milk. Serves two.

### Familia

2⅔ cups quick-cooking rolled oats
2⅔ cups quick-cooking rolled wheat
2 cups wheat germ
1 cup ground peanuts
1 cup sunflower seeds
¾ cup chopped peanuts
1 cup (or more) raisins
1 cup dried chopped apricots or peaches (or other fruit)

Mix ingredients. Serve with milk, yogurt, honey, or maple syrup. Makes 10 cups.
*Variations:*

**Camping familia**—Add one-third cup powdered milk for each cup of familia. Add hot or cold water.

**Fresh-fruit familia**—In spring and summer omit dried fruit and use fresh grapes, peaches, strawberries, or melon.

**Sesame familia**—Substitute sesame seeds for sunflower seeds.

**Traditional familia**—Use hazelnuts and almonds instead of sunflower seeds and peanuts.

### Fred's Potato Pancakes

This recipe is good for winter camping because it has nutritious vegetables as well as the fats you need in cold weather.

¾ cup dehydrated mixed vegetables
1 Tbsp. freeze-dried onions
1 Tbsp. potato flakes

Add first two ingredients to two cups cold water and let stand five minutes. Bring to a boil. Add potato flakes and stir, then remove from heat. Form mixture into patties and fry in butter until crisp on both sides. Makes six patties.

### Fresh-Fruit Breakfast

¼ cup ground walnuts
½ cup quick-cooking rolled oats
3 Tbsp. honey
1 cup yogurt
4 cups fruit or berries in season
juice of two lemons

At home, mix nuts and rolled oats and store in plastic. Mix honey with yogurt, and store in a plastic container. Wash fruit and store separately. In camp, slice fruit and cover with lemon juice. Add yogurt and dry ingredients, and mix well but gently. Serves five or six.

### Grilled Cheese Muffins

¼ cup butter
1 sourdough English muffin, halved
2 oz. cheese (any kind)
1 hardboiled egg (optional)

Butter muffin halves, place slices of cheese between halves and grill on hot griddle. Remove from grill and add slices of egg between muffin halves. Serves one.

## Grits And Eggs

> 6 Tbsp. quick-cooking grits
> ¼ cup dried egg powder
> 1¾ cups boiling water
> 1 or 2 Tbsp. butter
> ⅓ tsp. salt

Mix grits and egg powder, and add to boiling, buttered, salted water while stirring. Reduce heat, simmer three to five minutes, stirring occasionally. Add salt and pepper to taste.

## Hiker Cereal

> 3 cups oatmeal
> 1 cup wheat germ
> 1 cup chopped pecans
> 1 cup slivered almonds
> ¾ cup packed brown sugar

At home, mix ingredients and spread on cookie sheets. Toast in 250° F oven for an hour. Cool, and store in plastic bag. Chopped dried fruit can be added. Makes about six cups.

## Stewed Fruit Mix

> 6 oz. dried fruit (prunes, apricots, apples, raisins, etc.)
> 2 Tbsp. brown sugar
> dash of cinnamon, nutmeg, allspice

At home, chop fruit into small pieces, and store with brown sugar and spices in plastic bag. In camp, cover fruit with water, and simmer for 10 minutes or until tender and plump.

## Super Scramble

> 1 box dried hashbrowns with onions
> 2 Tbsp. oil or butter
> 3 oz. bacon bar or chopped salami
> 3 to 4 oz. chopped cheese

Cover potatoes with water to reconstitute. Drain, place in oiled frying pan and stir until slightly browned. Add crumbled bacon bar or salami and continue browning. Season, and add cheese, letting it melt on top. Serves two or three.

## Lunches And Snacks
## For On-The-Trail Nibbling

Because of the lengthy list of ingredients and the fact that you need an oven and/or other appliances, many of the following recipes require home preparation before hitting the trail.

### Backpacker's Delight

> 1 pound peanut butter
> 8 oz. honey
> ¼ cup powdered yeast
> ¼ cup soy bean lecithin
> ¼ cup condensed milk
> ¼ cup untoasted sesame seeds
> ¼ cup Chia seeds
> ¼ cup wheat germ
> ½ cup raisins or currants
> 1 cup mixed crushed nuts
> molasses, other nut butters, sunflower seeds (optional)

At home, mix ingredients and form into balls. Roll in nut meal, grated coconut, or wheat germ and store mixture in plastic bag.

### Backpacking Bars

> ¾ cup flour
> ½ cup quick-cooking rolled oats
> ½ cup softened butter
> ¼ cup toasted wheat germ
> 1 Tbsp. grated orange peel
> ½ cup packed brown sugar
> 2 eggs

¼ cup packed brown sugar
½ cup shredded coconut
4½ oz. slivered almonds

At home, mix first six ingredients into a bowl. Shape mixture into a ball and press into a greased eight-inch-square pan. Beat eggs with brown sugar. Stir in coconut and almonds. Pour this topping evenly over mixture in pan. Bake at 350° F for 25 minutes. Cool, and cut into bars. Wrap individually and store in refrigerator.

## Banana-Oat Energy Bars

¾ cup butter
1 cup packed brown sugar
1 egg
½ tsp. salt
1½ cups mashed ripe bananas (four or five)
4 cups quick-cooking rolled oats
1 cup raisins or chocolate chips
½ cup chopped walnuts or pecans

At home, cream butter and brown sugar until fluffy. Beat in egg, salt, and bananas. Stir in remaining ingredients. Turn into greased nine- by 13-inch pan. Bake at 350° F for one hour or until toothpick inserted in center comes out clean. Cool, and cut into bars. Wrap in plastic and store in refrigerator.

## Bannock

When the mountain men traveled, they carried little except coffee and flour for making bannock.

1 cup flour (can be whole wheat)
1 tsp. salt
2 Tbsp. oil or shortening

At home, mix flour and salt, then add oil or shortening and enough water to make a stiff dough. Form the dough into a ball, then flatten it to about an inch thick. Place in a greased frying pan and bake slowly over a low fire. Turn several times while cooking until the crust is brown and the inside is no longer sticky.

### Cannonballs

½ cup shortening
¾ cup packed brown sugar
1 large egg
1 tsp. vanilla
¼ cup milk
½ tsp. baking soda
¼ tsp. salt
1 cup whole wheat flour
¼ cup powdered milk
2 cups granola

At home, cream shortening and brown sugar. Mix in egg, vanilla and milk. Mix backing soda and salt with flour and add to creamed mixture. Stir in powdered milk and granola. The mixture will be stiff. Drop spoonfuls on greased cookie sheet. Bake at 350° F for 10 minutes. Mixture also can be rolled and shaped into a sausage about one inch thick, then frozen. Cut off slices one to two inches thick, and bake on a greased cookie sheet. Makes 18 to 24, depending on size.

### Canoe-Base Hudson Bay Bread

½ cup butter
¾ cup sugar
3 cups quick-cooking rolled oats
3 oz. honey
¼ cup raisins
¼ cup peanuts

At home, melt butter and add to sugar. Add half the rolled oats and mix. Heat honey, raisins, peanuts and the rest of the oats, and mix by hand. Place in a well-greased baking pan about ½ inch deep, and bake at 350° F for 25 to 30 minutes or until golden brown. Cool 10 minutes, then cut. Cool another 10 minutes, then flip the pan over to remove the bread. Let the bread cool completely before wrapping.

### Carob Candy

Carob looks like cocoa and tastes a bit like chocolate but has fewer calories. You can find it in most health-food stores.

½ cup carob powder
¼ cup wheat germ
¼ cup soy flour
½ cup sunflower seeds
½ cup sesame seeds
½ tsp. salt
½ cup honey
½ cup peanut butter
½ cup unsweetened grated coconut

At home, mix dry ingredients, then add honey and peanut butter. The mixture will be stiff and will require much kneading with a wooden spoon or hands. Form into ¾-inch balls and roll each ball in coconut. Makes 40 to 50 balls. Store in refrigerator.

### Carrot Bran Muffins

1½ cups whole wheat flour
1 tsp. salt
1½ tsp. baking soda
1½ cups bran
1 Tbsp. cinnamon
1½ cups milk
2 tsp. vinegar
¼ cup blackstrap molasses
⅓ cup honey
2 eggs
¼ cup oil
1 cup grated carrots
½ cup raisins or chopped nuts

At home, mix first five ingredients. Mix wet ingredients, and add carrots and raisins or nuts. Combine the dry and wet ingredients and mix until dry ingredients are moist. Don't beat too long! Fill buttered muffin tins two-thirds full. Bake at 375° F for 20 minutes. Makes about 24 muffins.

### Cheese And Dill Crackers

1 cup self-rising flour
½ cup quick-cooking rolled oats
½ cup wheat germ
⅓ cup sesame seeds

2 or 3 Tbsp. dill weed
1 tsp. salt
1 Tbsp. onion flakes
½ cup grated sharp cheddar cheese
¼ cup oil
¾ cup water

At home, mix dry ingredients and add cheese and oil. Blend thoroughly. Add water and stir until the mixture forms a thick dough. Spread the dough on a greased cookie sheet to a thickness of ¼ inch or less. Score lengthwise and crosswise in 1- to 1½-inch squares. Bake at 350° F about 45 minutes or until brown. Cool, break into squares, and return to warm oven to dry for two or three hours. Store in covered tin. Pack in plastic or foil for the trail.

### Chapatis

Chapatis are a type of unleavened flatbread, a Hindu variation on the same theme as tortillas, pocket bread, matzohs, even pizza. Chapatis are almost foolproof to make, keep well, and can be wrapped around virtually any food. All in all, an excellent trail food. The following recipe adds cornmeal to the traditional Hindu mix:

1½ cups whole wheat flour
½ cup cornmeal
milk

At home, mix flour and cornmeal. Add just enough milk to hold the dough together, then knead until smooth. Divide into golf-ball-sized pieces and roll out into round wafers as thin as possible, and store in plastic bag. In camp, heat frying pan over medium-high heat until a pinch of flour tossed into the pan smokes. Add no oil. Cook one chapati at a time, turning until lightly browned on each side. Move constantly to prevent burning. For crisper chapatis, cook longer. Top with tomato paste, cheese, meat, refried beans, or whatever you like. Also great with peanut butter, jelly, and honey.

### Creme De La Creme Loaf

1 pkg. (15 oz.) corn bread mix
⅛ cup wheat germ

1 cup flour
1 tsp. baking soda
1 tsp. baking powder
1 tsp. salt
½ cup raisins
¼ cup each chopped walnuts and cashews
½ cup chocolate chips (optional)
⅔ cup powdered milk
2 eggs, beaten
¾ cup applesauce
¼ cup maple syrup or honey
1 cup water

At home, mix dry ingredients. Add other ingredients and stir until thoroughly mixed. Pour into a nine- by five-inch loaf pan, or two three-and-a-half- by seven-inch loaf pans. Bake at 350° F for 30 minutes to one hour, depending on size of loaf pans. Cool, and wrap in foil or waxed paper.

### Date Halva

2 cups pitted dates
½ cup water
1 cup almonds
5 Tbsp. butter
¼ cup honey
1 tsp. ground cardamom

At home, chop dates in small pieces and soak in water 20 minutes until soft. Blend date mixture to a pulp and set aside. Chop almonds to consistency of coarse meal. Sauté almonds in butter and honey and stir until syruplike. When it bubbles, add date mixture. Stir six to eight minutes, add cardamom and mix well. Pour into a greased nine-inch-square pan and let cool. Cut into small pieces and wrap in plastic. Store in refrigerator.

### Four-Grain Granola

3 Tbsp. butter
½ cup packed brown sugar or honey
2 cups quick-cooking rolled oats
1 cup four-grain cereal (rye, oats, barley, wheat)
1 cup nuts and seeds (almonds, sunflower seeds)

½ cup raisins
½ cup chopped pitted dates or other dried fruit

At home, melt butter in a pan. Add brown sugar or honey, and stir until melted. Add oats and cereal, and fry until golden brown, stirring constantly. Mix in nuts and seeds, raisins, and fruit. Cool, and store in plastic bag in refrigerator. Makes eight cups.

### Fresno Bran Muffins

¾ cup milk
1 cup whole bran
2 Tbsp. shortening
⅓ cup sugar
1 egg, beaten
1 cup chopped dried figs
1 cup flour
1 Tbsp. baking powder
½ tsp. cinnamon
½ tsp. salt
¼ cup sugar

At home, pour milk over bran and let soak five minutes. Cream shortening with sugar. Add egg, bran mixture and figs. Sift flour with baking powder, cinnamon, and salt. Add to first mixture and blend well. Fill greased muffin pans two-thirds full. Sprinkle with remaining sugar. Bake at 375° F for 25 minutes. In camp, wrap muffins in foil and warm. Makes 12 muffins.

### Fry-Pan Bread

2 cups flour
3 tsp. baking powder
1 tsp. salt
6 Tbsp. butter
⅓ cup berries
⅓ cup water

At home, mix dry ingredients, then cut in butter until the mixture is the consistency of grain. Pour into plastic bag and store. (Do not keep longer than six weeks.) On the trail, mix with berries and water until the dough is easy to handle.

Shape into a cake one-inch thick that will fit into your frying pan, and dust with flour. Cook in the heated, greased pan over low heat until both sides are browned.

## Fudge Scotch Squares

> 1½ cups graham-cracker crumbs
> 1 can sweetened condensed milk
> 1 cup chocolate chips
> 1 cup butterscotch chips
> 1 cup coarsely chopped walnuts

At home, mix ingredients. Press mixture into a well-greased nine-inch-square pan. Bake at 350° F for 30 to 35 minutes. Cool for 45 minutes, cut into squares and remove from pan. If squares are not removed as soon as they cool, they stick to the pan.

## Gorp

Traditionally, gorp is granola, oats, raisins, and peanuts mixed and eaten along the trail. It's nutritious, lasts forever, and is virtually indestructible. Of course, you can make the mixture more creative by adding chocolate or carob chips or M&M's; dried fruits like apricots, banana chips, and apples; and seeds or nuts like sunflower seeds and corn nuts. Experiment!

## Gorp Cookies

> 1 cup butter
> 1½ cups honey
> 2 eggs, beaten
> ½ tsp. salt
> 2 tsp. vanilla
> 1 tsp. baking powder
> ¼ cup powdered milk
> 3¾ cups whole wheat flour
> 1 cup sunflower seeds
> 1½ cups chopped peanuts
> 1½ cups raisins
> 1½ cups chocolate or carob chips

At home, cream the butter until smooth. Beat in the honey,

then beat in eggs, salt and vanilla. In another bowl, mix baking powder, powdered milk, and flour; add it to the creamed mixture and blend. Stir in seeds, nuts, raisins, and chocolate or carob chips. Drop by teaspoons onto unoiled cookie sheets and bake at 375° F for 10 to 12 minutes.

### Granola (sugar free)

The following recipe uses neither sugar nor honey. Instead, the natural fruit sugar in unsweetened apple juice provides the sweetener.

> 1 can (12 oz.) unsweetened, concentrated
>   frozen apple juice
> ½ cup corn oil
> 2 tsp. vanilla
> 1½ cups shredded, unsweetened coconut
> 1 cup hulled sunflower seeds
> 1 cup soy flakes
> 4 cups quick-cooking rolled oats
> 1 cup wheat germ
> ½ cup each chopped almonds and pecans
> ½ cup bran
> ½ cup powdered milk
> ½ cup sesame seeds

At home, heat apple juice, corn oil, and vanilla in saucepan. Mix dry ingredients. Pour liquid over dry ingredients and mix well. Spread mixture on two cookie sheets and bake at 350° F for 15 minutes. Stir occasionally while baking. When done, granola will have a dry, cereal-like consistency. Eat dry as trail food or with milk for breakfast.

### Granola Bread

> ½ cup softened butter
> ¼ cup molasses
> ½ cup honey
> 1 egg
> 1 cup whole wheat flour
> ¾ cup bran
> 1 tsp. baking powder
> 1 tsp. baking soda
> ¼ tsp. salt

1 cup plain yogurt
1 cup granola
¼ cup raisins

At home, beat together butter, molasses, honey and egg. In another bowl, mix dry ingredients. Add to butter mixture along with yogurt, blending well. Mix in granola and raisins, and pour batter into greased loaf pan. Bake at 350° F for one hour or until done. For the trail, slice into single servings and wrap in plastic.

## *Grunch*

Tired of peanut butter? Then spruce it up!

1 cup chunky peanut butter
½ cup honey
½ cup crushed graham crackers
¼ cup powdered skim milk
3 Tbsp. cinnamon
1 Tbsp. powdered cloves

At home, mix ingredients. Store in plastic container and place in the refrigerator to harden overnight. Store in a plastic squeeze tube for easy carrying. Makes two cups.

## *Handy Candy*

3 Tbsp. peanut butter
1 pkg. (6 oz.) carob chips
18 pitted dates
½ tsp. grated orange peel
1 Tbsp. sesame seeds
⅓ cup coconut
2 Tbsp. honey

At home, blend all ingredients in a food processor, blender, or grinder until smooth. Roll small portions between hands, along with additional coconut and/or chopped nuts. Press into patties. Wrap in foil as you would a candy bar. The consistency remains stable whether refrigerated or not. Makes about 15 two-inch patties.

## Honey Bread

>    1 cup granulated sugar
>    1½ cups flour
>    1 cup whole wheat flour
>    1 tsp. baking soda
>    1 tsp. cinnamon
>    pinch of nutmeg
>    1 cup slivered almonds
>    ½ cup chopped dried apricots
>    ¾ cup honey
>    1 cup water

At home, mix dry ingredients. Put honey in large bowl and add dry ingredients. Mix well and add water. Line a loaf pan with waxed paper and fill two-thirds full with the mixture. Bake at 350° to 375° F for 90 minutes. Allow to cool before removing from pan.

## Jerky

>    1½ lbs. beef (or venison, chicken, turkey, or ham)
>    1 tsp. seasoned salt
>    1 tsp. onion powder
>    ½ tsp. garlic powder
>    ½ tsp. pepper
>    ½ cup Worcestershire sauce
>    ½ cup soy sauce

At home, remove fat from meat. Cut into ¼-inch slices along grain. The thinner the meat, the faster it dries. It is easier to slice if partially frozen. Combine dry and wet ingredients to make marinade. Marinate meat overnight in refrigerator. Drain. Lay meat strips on oven rack and place foil on bottom rack to catch drippings. Leave door ajar. Set oven at 150° F. Dry meat for five hours. Turn oven off, turn strips over and leave in oven for another five hours. Store jerky in covered container with holes punched in lid. Makes one pound.

## Logan Bread

This classic bread is highly nutritious, travels well, and can be eaten at any time. It has low moisture content and will keep for months if properly stored. Freeze or keep in cloth bag in a dry place. What isn't used on one hike will easily carry over to the next.

> 3 cups flour (2 cups rye, 1 cup whole wheat)
> ¾ cup wheat germ
> ¼ cup packed brown sugar
> ½ cup powdered milk
> ½ cup chopped walnuts or pecans
> ½ cup raisins
> ½ cup chopped dried peaches, apricots, or dates
> 2 Tbsp. oil
> ½ cup honey
> ¼ cup molasses
> ¼ cup maple syrup
> 6 eggs

At home, mix flour, wheat germ, brown sugar, milk, nuts, raisins, and dried fruit. Beat in oil, honey, molasses, syrup, and eggs. The mixture should be heavier than bread dough. Press into one-inch-deep oiled pans. Bake at 275° F for two hours or until done.

### Molasses Hardtack

> 1 tsp. baking soda
> ⅔ cup water
> 2 eggs
> 2 cups molasses
> ⅔ cup melted shortening
> 1 tsp. powdered ginger
> 5½ cups whole wheat flour
> 1 cup raisins

At home, dissolve baking soda in water. Place in large bowl, and add eggs, molasses, shortening, and ginger. Mix well. Add flour and raisins. Mixture should be stiff. Roll one heaping tablespoon of dough in flour until it is five inches long. Place on cookie sheet and flatten with spatula. Roll and flatten rest of dough. Bake in 350° F oven about 15 minutes. Store in plastic bag. Makes 18 to 20 biscuits.

### Molasses Nut Bars

> ½ cup molasses and/or honey

1 cup powdered milk
½ cup chunky peanut butter
½ cup raisins

At home, mix all ingredients and turn onto waxed paper sprinkled with powdered milk. Knead, and add more powdered milk until mixture loses its stickiness. Pat down until ½ inch thick, and cut into sticks. Wrap in plastic and store in refrigerator.

## Mountain Bars

2 cups whole wheat flour
½ tsp. salt
2 Tbsp. packed brown sugar
⅓ cup chopped walnuts
¼ cup oil or melted butter
⅓ cup cold water
⅓ cup honey

At home, mix the dry ingredients and drip oil or butter over them. Mix well and pour in water and honey. Mix into a stiff dough. Knead on board and press out by hand until ¼-inch thick. Cut into ½- by three-inch pieces, place on a greased cookie sheet, and bake at 325° F for 30 minutes. Turn over once during baking.

## Munchie Cubes

2 (8 oz.) unsweetened chocolate bars
1¼ cups raisins
1¼ cups Spanish peanuts
1¼ cups Rice Krispies

At home, melt the chocolate slowly in a double boiler. Add other ingredients slowly, and stir continuously until everything is coated with chocolate. Spoon mixture into plastic ice cube trays and press mixture down gently. Freeze for 15 minutes. Makes about 30 cubes.

## Nut Cheese Loaf

1 cup water
½ cup brown rice

2 cups chopped onions
2 tsp. oil
1½ cups grated cheddar cheese
1 cup ground walnuts, pecans, or other nuts
3 eggs, beaten

At home, boil water and cook rice. Sauté onions in oil. Add all ingredients to rice, and mix. Pour into a loaf pan and bake at 350° F for 30 minutes. Cool, cut in one-inch slices, and wrap in plastic or foil. May be eaten cold or warmed in foil.

### Nutty Wheat Balls

1 cup water
2 cups Cream of Wheat
2 cups chunky peanut butter
1 cup honey
¼ cup walnuts
¼ cup raisins
¼ cup chocolate chips

At home, boil water and cook Cream of Wheat. Melt peanut butter and honey in saucepan and add to Cream of Wheat. Add nuts, raisins, and chocolate chips. Spoon onto waxed paper and allow to cool until hard.

### Oatcakes

This hearty snack comes from the Scotch Highlands, where the inhabitants use oats as a protein-rich meat substitute.

4 cups quick-cooking rolled oats
1 cup whole wheat flour
1 tsp. salt
1 tsp. baking soda
3 Tbsp. butter
boiling water

At home, mix dry ingredients. Cut in butter. Isolate small portion of mixture at the edge of the bowl. Add one table-spoon water to this portion and stir. Repeat with rest of mixture until cohesive. Beware of adding too much water. Roll out onto a floured board until thin. Cut into two-inch squares and bake at 350° F for 20 to 25 minutes or until brown. Turn once. Cool, and store in refrigerator in plastic bag.

### Peanut Butter Bread

    1 cup peanut butter
    2 cups flour
    1 cup sugar
    1 tsp. salt
    2 tsp. baking powder
    1 egg
    1 cup milk

    At home, mix the peanut butter into the dry ingredients. In a separate bowl, beat egg into milk. Add to peanut butter mixture and mix gently. Do not beat. (The batter may be slightly lumpy.) Pour into a greased pan and bake at 350° F for one hour.

### Peanut Butter Cookies

    These cookies crumble less than most and keep their flavor for weeks.

    1 can (15 oz.) sweetened condensed milk
    ½ cup peanut butter
    ½ tsp. lemon juice
    ¼ tsp. salt
    1 tsp. vanilla
    1 cup chopped peanuts

    At home, mix ingredients. Drop teaspoons of batter on buttered cookie sheet. Bake at 375° F for 10 minutes. You can substitute a cup of raisins or chopped nuts for the peanuts.

### Peanut Polka Dotties

    1½ cups quick-cooking rolled oats
    1 can (15 oz.) sweetened condensed milk
    ½ tsp. salt
    1 tsp. vanilla
    ½ cup chunky peanut butter
    1 bag (12 oz.) chocolate chips

    At home, mix oats, milk, salt and vanilla. Stir in peanut butter and chocolate chips. Press into eight-inch-square pan. Bake at 350° F for 30 minutes.

### Pemmican

Make a modern version of the old buffalo meat and berry combination.

    ½ cup each raisins, dried apricots, and dates
    ½ cup dried beef
    ½ cup grated orange peel
    ¾ cup packed brown sugar
    ½ to 1 tsp. each cinnamon, nutmeg, and allspice
    pinch of salt
    1 tsp. vanilla
    1 Tbsp. each vinegar, oil, and maple syrup
    ½ beaten egg
    ½ cup flour
    Cider, rum, or brandy

At home, chop fine or put through blender raisins, dried fruit, and beef, then mix in remaining ingredients. Add enough cider, rum, or brandy to make a heavy dough. Bake in a nine-inch-square pan at 325° F at least 1 hour until it sets well and isn't too sticky.

### Pemmican Fruit Bars

    1 lb. dried pitted dates
    4 oz. dried apricots
    4 oz. pitted prunes
    4 oz. candied pineapple
    4 oz. golden raisins
    ¼ cup grated coconut
    1 cup chopped mixed nuts

At home, chop together fruit and stir all ingredients together, then run the mixture through a meat grinder using the coarsest outlet available. A sticky mess will result. Dust a cookie sheet liberally with powdered sugar. Using the bottom of a large spoon, mash the mixture into a flat, solid slab on the cookie sheet. Cut into bars and dust each with more sugar. Let dry for a few weeks, if you have time and can resist temptation. Wrap individually in foil.

### Pioneer Bread

> 2 cups whole wheat flour
> 2 cups unbleached white flour
> 1 tsp. baking soda
> 1 tsp. salt
> 1 cup raisins
> 2 Tbsp. caraway seeds
> ½ cup butter
> ½ cup honey
> 3 eggs
> 1 cup buttermilk

At home, mix dry ingredients. Cream together butter, honey, eggs, and buttermilk. Combine all ingredients, mix well, and place in a greased loaf pan. Bake at 375° F 50 to 60 minutes. It's done when the sides of the loaf start to shrink away from the pan and a toothpick inserted in the center comes out clean.

### Roman Rusk

Rusk was first used by the Roman legions as rations while on the march. When the Roman Empire spread, so did the consumption of rusk. A simple rusk can be made by mixing honey and flour.

> ½ cup honey
> 1 cup flour

At home, mix the honey and flour. Spread the batter into thin biscuits on a cookie sheet. Bake at 350° F about 15 minutes until dark brown.

### Salami

> 2½ tsp. garlic salt or powder
> 2½ tsp. mustard seeds
> 1½ tsp. peppercorns
> 2½ tsp. hickory-smoked salt
> 2 Tbsp. oregano or other herbs
> 5 lbs. ground beef

At home, mix seasonings thoroughly into meat and roll mixture into a ball. Cover and refrigerate overnight. On the second, third, and fourth days, knead well, and replace in refrigerator. On the fifth day, divide mixture into 10 portions and form each into a tightly rolled log about two inches in diameter. Lay the logs on a rack in a shallow pan and dry in a 150° F oven for eight to 10 hours. Remove logs from oven and cool on paper towels to absorb remaining fat. Roll in plastic wrap or foil and store in freezer. Seasoning varies depending of preference; add more garlic salt or powder and herbs, if you like.

### Sesame Date Bars

> 1½ cups quick-cooking rolled oats
> 1½ cups sesame seeds
> 1½ cups powdered milk
> 1½ cups pitted dates
> ¾ cup packed brown sugar or honey
> 2 tsp. vanilla
> ½ cup water

At home, toast oats and sesame seeds in a heavy skillet. Mix in bowl with powdered milk, dates and brown sugar or honey. Stir in the flavoring. Add water until the batter is sticky and stiff enough to hold together. Press evenly into a shallow pan, and bake at 250° F for about 90 minutes. Cut into bars, cool, wrap each in plastic, and freeze.

### Spiced Pecans

> 2 Tbsp. butter
> 1 cup pecan halves
> 1 Tbsp. soy sauce
> 2 dashes hot-pepper sauce
> ¼ tsp. seasoned salt

At home, melt butter in shallow pan. Spread nuts evenly in one layer and bake at 300° F for 20 minutes, stirring often to prevent burning. When nuts begin to brown, combine remaining ingredients and pour over nuts, coating them well. Bake five minutes longer. Cool, and store in refrigerator in plastic bag.

### Texas Spiced Pecans

>1 cup sugar
>1 tsp. salt
>½ tsp. each nutmeg and cloves
>2 tsp. cinnamon
>¼ cup water
>½ lb. pecan halves

At home, blend all ingredients except pecans in saucepan, and cook over medium heat, stirring constantly, until a drop of the syrup forms a tiny ball when placed in cold water. Add pecans to syrup. Remove syrup from heat and stir gently until the mixture is sugary. Spread on waxed paper and cool until hardened. Break into pieces, and store in plastic bag.

### Tortillas

>2 cups whole wheat flour
>½ tsp. salt
>1 Tbsp. corn oil
>water

At home, mix flour and salt, then mix in oil. Add water until a soft dough is formed. Add more flour if dough is too sticky. Knead five minutes until well mixed. Form into one-and-a half-inch balls and roll on floured board until as thin as possible. Fry in lightly oiled skillet until tortilla bubbles, then turn and brown the other side. Cool, and store in plastic bag.

### White Mountain Survival Bread

>2 cups applesauce
>2 cups chopped pitted dates
>1¼ cups water
>8 oz. cream cheese
>¾ cup peanut butter
>½ cup chopped sunflower seeds
>1 cup wheat germ
>½ cup sesame seeds
>4 eggs
>1 Tbsp. salt
>1 cup powdered milk
>2 cups quick-cooking rolled oats
>3 cups flour

At home, mix applesauce, dates, and water, and heat until dates are soft. Remove from heat and add remaining ingredients. Spread one-half inch thick in shallow pans. Bake at 350° F for 25 minutes or until done.

### Wilderness Logs

>  2 cups peanut butter
>  1 cup crushed cookies (vanilla wafers, ginger snaps)
>  ¾ cup chopped nuts
>  1 cup chocolate chips
>  ½ cup honey
>  ¼ lb. chopped pitted dates and raisins
>  ½ cup shredded coconut
>  ¼ tsp. each cinnamon and nutmeg

At home, mix ingredients together. Knead well, adding a tablespoon of water if mixture is too dry. Roll into one- by four-inch logs, and wrap each in foil or plastic wrap. Store in freezer until ready to use. Makes 10 to 12 rolls.

### Zucchini Bread

This moist, nutritious bread can be baked in coffee cans, so it's easy to carry on the trail (right in the can). Although the bread doesn't taste like zucchini, it satisfies the craving for green and yellow vegetables some folks get after several days on the trail.

>  1 cup sugar
>  1 cup packed brown sugar
>  1 cup oil
>  3 eggs
>  2 cups grated zucchini
>  3 tsp. vanilla
>  3 cups sifted flour
>  1 tsp. salt
>  1 tsp. baking soda
>  3 tsp. cinnamon
>  ¼ tsp. baking powder
>  ½ cup chopped nuts

At home, mix sugars, oil, and eggs. Beat until blended. Add zucchini and vanilla. In a separate bowl, mix flour, salt, baking soda, cinnamon, and baking powder. Blend well with creamed mixture. Add nuts. Pour into two greased, lightly floured loaf pans. Bake at 325° F for one hour or until tooth-pick inserted in center comes out clean. If making in coffee cans, add 15 or 20 minutes onto baking time.

## Dinners—Menus
## For Watching The Sun Set

### Baked Onion

A potato wrapped in aluminum foil and baked over coals is an old-time camp treat. Also delicious is a whole onion cooked the same way. When wrapping either, make sure the shiny side of the foil is turned inward. The dull side absorbs heat more efficiently, and when facing outward will reduce baking time.

### Beef Barley Soup

1 pkg. beef barley soup mix
½ cup instant barley
1 tsp. onion flakes
1 beef bouillon cube
2 Tbsp. dried vegetable mix (optional)
2 or 3 dried mushrooms, broken into pieces
4 cups water

At home, mix all dry ingredients and store in plastic bag. In camp, boil water. Add ingredients from bag and simmer for 10 minutes until vegetables are soft. Serves two.

### Beef Soup

2 Tbsp. chopped onions
1 Tbsp. parsley
1 2-oz. meat bar
2 cups water
1 pkg. beef-flavored Ramen noodles

Add onions, parsley, and meat bar (broken into small pieces) to water, and bring mixture to boil. Break noodles into small pieces, add to water and bring to boil. Cook three to five minutes and stir in flavor packet that comes with noodles. Serves one to two.

### Breaded Surprise

> 3 cups cubed bread
> ⅓ tsp. garlic powder
> ⅔ cup oil
> 2 large onions
> ½ cup bacon bits
> 1 cup grated cheese

Fry bread with garlic powder in ⅓ cup oil until crisp. Set aside. Slice onions and separate into rings. Sauté onions in remaining oil. Drain oil, then add bacon bits, cheese, and bread cubes. Stir until mixture is warm.

### Bulghur

Also known as bulgur or burghul, this dish has long been a staple of Middle Eastern farmers and nomads. Whole wheat grains are parboiled and dried, the bran is removed and the kernels are cracked into fine, medium, or coarse particles or left whole. Parboiling precooks the wheat; it only need be warmed and rehydrated to be ready to eat. The rich, nutty flavor combines well with fruits, vegetables, cheeses, fish, and meat. It may be eaten hot or cold.

Bulghur can be found in health-food stores and some supermarkets. For preparation, two volumes of water are required to one volume of grain, and a half cup grain will provide about two cups reconstituted bulghur.

The following five recipes use bulghur:

### Bulghur With Fruit And Nuts

> 1 tsp. salt
> 2 cups water
> 1 cup finely ground bulghur
> ½ cup nuts, raisins, and/or berries

Add salt to water and bring to boil. Stir in bulghur, nuts, raisins, and/or berries. Lower heat, cover and cook for one

minute. Remove from heat and let stand five to 10 minutes.
Serve with brown sugar and milk.

### Bulghur Stew

    ¾ cup bulghur
    1 pkg. tomato soup mix
    1 pkg. onion soup mix
    ¼ cup powdered milk
    1 tsp. garlic powder
    1 tsp. salt
    2 cups water
    2 oz. chopped cheese
    2 to 3 Tbsp. sunflower or sesame seeds

At home, mix first six ingredients. In camp, bring water to a
boil and add dry ingredients. Lower heat, cover, and cook
about 20 minutes. Remove from heat, and stir in cheese and
sunflower or sesame seeds. Adding chopped vegetables
makes a heartier stew. Serves two.

### Green Mountain Stew

    3 cups water
    ¾ cup bulghur
    ¾ cup dehydrated peas
    1 can (5 oz.) Vienna sausages

Add water to bulghur and peas. Bring to a boil and cook 10
to 15 minutes or until all water is absorbed. Add sausages five
minutes before cooking is over, and stir. Serves two.

### Tuna Bulghur

    1½ cups bulghur
    1 tsp. onion salt
    1 tsp. parsley flakes
    ½ tsp. thyme
    ½ tsp. basil
    1 can (6½ oz.) tuna
    3 cups water
    1 vegetable bouillon cube
    2 pkg. cream of mushroom soup mix

At home, mix first five ingredients. In camp, soak the mixture for several minutes in the juice from the tuna. Add water, bouillon, and soup mix. Cover and heat until all the liquid is absorbed, about 15 minutes. Stir in tuna. Serves four.

### Weetamoo Stew

> 1 cup instant rice
> ½ cup bulghur
> ¼ cup cashew pieces
> 2 Tbsp. dried green vegetables
> ¼ cup dried mushrooms
> 1 pkg. cream of mushroom soup mix
> 1 tsp. garlic powder
> 1 tsp. salt
> ½ tsp. pepper
> 4 cups water
> 2 Tbsp. butter

At home, combine all ingredients except water and butter and store in plastic bag. In camp, add ingredients to water after bringing it to a boil. Lower heat, cover and cook 15 to 20 minutes. Add butter and serve. Dried beef may be added if meat is desired. Serves four.

### Cashew Rice Curry

> ¼ cup powdered milk
> ½ tsp. salt
> 1 or 2 tsp. curry powder
> 2½ cups water
> 1 cup rice
> ¼ cup cashew pieces
> 2 oz. grated cheddar cheese

Mix the powdered milk and seasonings with a little water to form a paste. Add the rest of the water, mix well and bring to a boil. Stir in rice, cover and simmer about 20 minutes until the liquid is absorbed and the rice is soft. Stir in nuts and cheese. Serve when cheese melts. Serves two or three.

### Chicken Rice Amandine

> 1 can (6 oz.) chicken (or tuna)
> 3½ cups water

3½ cups instant rice
½ tsp. onion salt
½ tsp. celery salt
2 tsp. onion flakes
3 oz. slivered almonds
2 pkgs. cream of chicken soup mix
⅔ cup raisins (optional)

Place chicken and water in pot and bring to a boil. Add rice and other ingredients and bring to a boil. Cover, remove from heat, and let stand for 10 minutes. Serves four.

### Chicken And Stuffing

2 cups water
¼ cup onion flakes
1 Tbsp. celery flakes
½ cup chopped dried mushrooms
2 (6 oz.) cans chicken
1 bag stuffing mix with herbs and spices

Bring water to a boil, add onions, celery, mushrooms and chicken. Break chicken into small chunks. Add stuffing mix. Remove from heat and mix well. Serves four to six.

### Chicken Sauce And Noodles

6 cups water
3 oz. soy protein
2 cups egg noodles
1 Tbsp. chopped dried mushrooms
2 pkgs. cream of chicken soup mix
¼ tsp. pepper
2 tsp. chicken bouillon powder
1 tsp. onion flakes

Bring water to boil. Add soy protein, noodles, and mushrooms and boil seven minutes. Drain off most of liquid, reserving one cup of it. Return cup of liquid to noodle mixture. Add remaining ingredients. Cook slowly another five minutes. Serves three.

### Chili Sauce

Here is a quick and easy way to spice up eggs or other dishes.

> tomato soup mix
> dry peppers
> celery flakes
> onion flakes
> chili powder

At home, mix ingredients, and store in a plastic bag. Adjust the proportions to suit your taste. In camp, add water to the mixture.

### Coastline Stew

If you're able to catch or gather fish or shellfish, this recipe gives you a seafood alternative.

> 4½ cups water
> ¼ cup onion flakes
> ¼ cup vegetable flakes
> ½ cup butter
> ½ cup tomato base
> 1 Tbsp. oregano
> ¾ cup pearl barley
> fish or shellfish

Bring water to boil. Add all ingredients except fish and simmer. In another covered pan with ½ inch water, steam the fish, then add to the stew and continue simmering until barley and vegetables are soft.

### Couscous

Couscous is a delicious and easy-to-prepare addition to any backpacking menu. It consists of tiny dry pellets of crushed grain that expand and absorb moisture when cooked in boiling water. The result is a cross between pasta and rice. You can make terrific pilafs by adding onions, herbs, bouillon, meats, or whatever. Total cooking time is only about 15 minutes. Couscous is available in the rice/pasta sections of many supermarkets. Cooking instructions are on the package.

## Cream Soup

This is a generic recipe for cream soup. Add to it whatever's on hand or whatever your imagination conjures up. The fun's in the experimentation. To six cups boiling water, add three tablespoon flavor base (mushroom, beef, chicken, etc.) and one cup "soup solids," such as dried vegetables, lentils, noodles, rice, etc. Cook until solids are done, then add three tablespoons butter, and thicken with potato flakes or flour. Add a half cup powdered milk and a half cup water. Season to taste.

## Curried Chicken

1 oz. mixed celery, onion, and pepper flakes
2 cups water
½ pkg. vegetable soup mix
½ pkg. curry sauce mix or 1 Tbsp. curry powder
⅛ tsp. or more cayenne pepper
⅔ cup instant rice
3 Tbsp. powdered milk
1 can (6 oz.) chicken
2 oz. shredded coconut
2 oz. raisins

Soak vegetables in water. Add soup mix and seasonings. Bring to a boil. Stir in rice, milk, and chicken. Simmer 10 minutes. Serve topped with coconut and raisins. Serves two.

## Curried Mushrooms

1 oz. sliced dried mushrooms
1 cup water
2 oz. curry seasoning mix or 3 Tbsp. curry powder
2 pkgs. beef, chicken, or pork Ramen noodles

Soak mushrooms in the water for 20 minutes. Pour mushroom water in another pan, adding enough water to make four-and-a-half cups. Bring to boil. Add curry and noodles. Boil for three minutes, stirring occasionally. Remove from heat and stir in seasoning mix from noodle package. Serve immediately. Serves two.

### *Curried Vegetables*

> 2 pkgs. vegetable soup mix
> 4½ cups water
> 3 cups instant rice
> 1 Tbsp. curry powder
> 5 oz. raisins
> 3 oz. chopped nuts
> 2 oz. shredded coconut

Mix vegetable soup with water. Bring to boil. Add rice and stir. Turn off stove, then add curry powder, raisins, and nuts. Cover pot. Wait five minutes, then sprinkle coconut on top and serve. Serves four.

### *Devil's Thumb Stew*

> 4 cups water
> 1 pkg. vegetable beef soup mix
> 1 box (7¼ oz.) macaroni and cheese dinner
> 1 can (6½ oz.) tuna
> ½ cup instant rice

Bring water to boil. Add soup mix and macaroni. Simmer until macaroni is about half done. Add cheese and tuna, then enough rice to obtain desired consistency. Cook until macaroni and rice are done. Serves four.

### *Dumplings*

> 1 cup whole wheat flour
> 1 cup white flour
> 2 tsp. baking powder
> 1 tsp. salt
> 2 Tbsp. shortening or oil
> ¼ cup powdered milk

At home, mix ingredients. In camp, add three tablespoons water per half cup of mix and combine well. Spoon into boiling stew or soup. Cook 10 minutes uncovered and 10 minutes covered.

## Enchiladas

>    1 cup cornmeal
>    ½ cup biscuit mix
>    ½ cup water
>    2 Tbsp. butter
>    ½ cup tomato base
>    ½ cup water
>    ¼ cup onion flakes
>    ¼ tsp. chili powder
>    dash of tabasco
>    salt and pepper to taste
>    ½ cup cheese

Mix first three ingredients. Shape the cornmeal mixture into flat patties and fry in butter until soft-crisp. Then make the sauce by mixing remaining ingredients. Pour the sauce over the patties, fold the patties in half, then top them with cheese. Bake over coals in frying pan until cheese starts to bubble.

## Green Pea Soup

If you can remember to soak the peas all day, your reward will be a hearty and filling split pea soup for dinner. This is a good recipe for those days you don't break camp.

>    2 cups split peas
>    4 cups water
>    salt and pepper to taste
>    handful of onion flakes
>    handful of ham or bacon bits

Rinse peas well and soak them in water all day. Boil until soft. Add spices, onion flakes, and ham or bacon bits, and simmer until thick. The longer you simmer, the thicker it gets.

## Grits Au Gratin

>    2⅔ cups water
>    ½ tsp. salt
>    ⅔ cup quick-cooking grits
>    4 oz. chopped cheddar cheese
>    ¼ tsp. pepper
>    1 can (4½ oz.) drained shrimp
>    ¼ cup butter

Bring water to a boil. Add salt and grits. Return to a boil, add cheese and pepper and stir until cheese melts. Lower heat, add shrimp and cook about five minutes until the mixture thickens. Top with a serving of butter. Serves four.

## Protein-Rich Legumes

Dried beans and lentils have long been staples of agricultural civilizations. The pottage Jacob provided his brother Esau in return for Esau's birthright was a lentil stew. Bean of lentil porridge was common fare in Middle Eastern cultures 4,000 years ago. Early European and Asian civilizations also relied on these protein-rich legumes. In modern times, as meat eating increased, the reputation of dried beans (red, navy, pinto, lima, soy, and lentils) suffered when they became associated with foods of the poor. Their popularity has been restored somewhat by vegetarians. Try drying your own beans, and then using them in the following recipes.

### *Dried Beans*

At home, put one pound of dried beans—any kind—in a pressure cooker without the rack. Add water two inches above level of beans. Pressure cook for 30 minutes as directed by pressure-cooker instructions. Drain well, spread in a single layer on cookie sheets, and dry in the oven at lowest heat until dry and hard. Ovens vary; it will take 12 hours with a gas-oven pilot only or about six hours at 140° F, and about the same time in an electric oven at its lowest setting. You can also use a home dehydrator.

For the trail, measure desired amount of beans, and store in plastic bag with onion flakes, tomato flakes, bouillon cubes, bacon bits, or any other vegetable or seasoning. In camp, soak the mixture 10 minutes, bring water to boil, and cook for 10 to 15 minutes until done.

### *Lentil And Rice Casserole*

> 1 cup lentils
> 1 cup brown rice
> ¼ cup onion flakes
> 1 cup dried tomatoes

garlic powder to taste
chicken bouillon, enough to make 4 cups
1 tsp. cumin
4 cups water
¼ cup butter

Pour all ingredients except water and butter into a skillet. Add water, stir, and bring to boil. Lower heat, cover, and let mixture simmer 45 minutes or until rice is tender. Stir in butter and serve. Serves four.

## Lentil Stew

2 cups lentils
½ cup sesame seeds
¼ cup pumpkin or sunflower seeds
¼ cup dried potatoes or potato flakes
¼ cup powdered milk
½ cup textured vegetable protein (TVP), any flavor
¼ cup onion flakes
2 tsp. salt
1 crushed bay leaf
4 cups water

At home, mix dry ingredients and store in plastic bag. In camp, add mixture to boiling water and simmer 20 to 25 minutes. Serves four.

## Meatless Goulash

½ cup dried lentils
½ cup split peas
½ cup soy granules
2 cups bulghur or brown buckwheat groats
5 Tbsp. brewer's yeast
5 Tbsp. powdered milk
2 Tbsp. quick-cooking rolled oats
1½ cups water

At home, put lentils and split peas in a blender and grind to a meallike consistency. Combine with remaining dry ingredients. Store in an airtight container. To reconstitute in camp, add ⅔ cup of mixture to water. Bring to a boil, stirring occasionally. Simmer five to 10 minutes or until water is absorbed. Two-thirds cup provides one large serving or two small ones.

### Spicy Lentils

⅔ cup lentils
⅓ cup short-grain brown rice
1 Tbsp. sesame seeds
2 pinches of cayenne pepper
2 pinches of cumin
¼ tsp. curry powder
¼ tsp. salt
2 cups water

At home, mix dry ingredients and store in plastic bag. On the trail, add water and simmer until the water has been absorbed and lentils are soft. Serve on bread, crackers, or tortillas.

### Mexaroni

2¼ cups elbow macaroni
1 pkg. taco sauce mix
¼ cup powdered milk
¼ cup dried vegetable mix
Salt and cayenne pepper to taste
5 cups water
½ cup grated Parmesan cheese

At home, mix dry ingredients except cheese, and store in plastic bag. In camp, pour mixture in pot and add the water. Stir until well mixed and bring to a boil. Cover, and simmer until macaroni is done. Mix in cheese just before serving, or add to each serving as a topping.

**Pasta hint:** For this and other macaroni or noodle dishes, try using just enough water to allow the pasta to rehydrate fully. Backpacking pots are small, water may be scarce, and valuable nutrients are poured away when you drain cooked pasta. A lid of foil cuts cooking time, saves fuel, and prevents evaporation. When pasta is done al dente (slightly resistant to the bite), add the rest of your ingredients. This method allows you to add spices and bouillon while the noodles are cooking.

### Mushroom Soy Stew

½ cup dried vegetable mix
4 cups water
½ cup soy protein, any flavor
2 pkgs. cream of mushroom soup
butter
salt and pepper to taste

Soak dried vegetables in one cup of water about 30 minutes until the liquid is absorbed. Boil remaining water and add vegetables. Cook for about five minutes. Take pot off stove, mix in soy protein and mushroom soup mix, and let stand five minutes. Add butter, salt, and pepper if desired. Serves two.

### Nut Soup

4 cups water
3 oz. uncooked spinach noodles
¾ cup instant rice
1 pkg. chicken noodle soup mix
1 Tbsp. chicken bouillon
¾ cup toasted slivered almonds
¾ cup raisins

Boil water, and add noodles, rice, soup mix, and bouillon. Cook eight minutes. Add more water if needed. Stir in almonds and raisins, and serve. Makes five cups.

### Oyster Chowder

1 can smoked oysters
1 pkg. onion soup mix
1½ cups potato flakes
4 cups water
1 pkg. sour cream soup mix
1½ Tbsp. powdered milk
½ cup water

Mix oysters, onion soup, and potato flakes with water, and bring to a boil. Simmer 10 minutes. In another pot, mix remaining ingredients with rest of water. Add to chowder mix, stir and serve.

## Pasta Al Carbonara

¾ lb. elbow macaroni or spaghetti
3 tsp. salt
4 cups water
2 pkgs. powdered egg
⅓ cup grated Parmesan cheese
1½ Tbsp. parsley flakes
3 Tbsp. butter
⅓ cup imitation bacon bits

Boil pasta in salted water until tender. Mix egg with cold water until smooth. Beat cheese and parsley flakes into egg and water until blended. Drain macaroni, stir in butter until macaroni is well coated, and add cheese and egg mixture. Top with bacon bits.

## Pea Soup With Ham

2 pkgs. pea soup mix
6 cups water
1 pkg. bouillon (optional)
1 pkg. freeze-dried ham

Mix and simmer 10 minutes. Serves three to four.

## Pemigewasset Stew

¾ cup millet
¼ cup chick peas (garbanzo beans)
¾ cup dried vegetable mix
3½ cups water

Add ingredients to boiling water. Bring to a boil and cook 10 to 15 minutes until water is absorbed and mixture is tender. Serve with butter and salt. Millet and chick peas can be found in health-food stores. Serves two.

## Refried Beans

2 cups precooked dried beans
1 tsp. salt
4 tsp. oil
1 bacon bar (optional)
4 oz. grated cheese (optional)

Soak beans 30 minutes in salted water to cover, then bring
to a boil. Simmer until tender and water is absorbed. Put
beans in a frying pan with oil and stir and mash with a fork. If
too dry, add a bit more water. For additional flavor, add a
crumbled bacon bar or cheese and mix well.

### Rice And Meal

> 1 tsp. salt
> 4 cups water
> 1 cup cornmeal
> 1 cup water
> 3 oz. bacon bits
> 2 cups instant rice

Add salt to water and bring to boil. Mix cornmeal with one
cup water and add to the boiling pot, stirring briskly. Boil for
five minutes. Stir in bacon bits and instant rice. Cover, remove
from heat, and let stand for 10 minutes. Serves four.

### Slate Lake Chicken With Rice

> 1 cup instant brown rice
> ¼ cup slivered almonds
> ¼ cup dried mushrooms or one can (6 oz.)
> 2 Tbsp. onion flakes
> 1 Tbsp. dried green or red pepper
> ½ tsp. salt
> 1½ cups water
> 2 pkgs. dried chicken or 2 cans (6 oz.) chicken
> 2 pkgs. cream of chicken soup mix
> sage (optional)

Simmer the first seven ingredients for 15 minutes. Add
remaining ingredients. If using dried chicken, increase water
by almost a cup and add the chicken with rice. If using
canned chicken, add it and soup after 15 minutes. Stir well
and heat several more minutes. Otherwise, just add soup and
seasoning. Serves four.

### Spicy Spaghetti Sauce

> 1½ cups cubed cheddar cheese
> 1 cup tomato base and enough water to make a paste

1 tsp. oregano
½ tsp. garlic powder
2 Tbsp. onion flakes or 1 Tbsp. onion powder
1½ cups raisins
½ cup bacon bits
wheat germ

Melt cheese into tomato sauce, then add spices, raisins, bacon bits, and enough wheat germ to thicken if necessary. Simmer and serve over almost anything—fish, rice, noodles.

### Sweet And Sour Fried Rice

2 oz. dried vegetable mix
2 to 3 oz. dried chicken, beef, or pork
3 cups water
1 cup instant rice
1 pkg. fried rice mix
1 pkg. sweet and sour sauce mix
3 Tbsp. soy sauce
½ tsp. Chinese Five Spice

Soak vegetables and meat in one cup water. Add rice and rice mix to remaining boiling water. Simmer five minutes. Remove from heat and let stand for five minutes. Add sweet and sour sauce mix, soy sauce, and seasonings to meat and vegetable mix. Heat to boiling. Serve meat and vegetables on rice. Serves two.

### Trout

If you're in the right place and have the patience and fishing gear, adding fresh trout to an evening meal is a treat. Try these next three recipes. Of course, other fish will do, and canned tuna works, too.

### Pineapple Trout

1 pkg. freeze-dried pineapple
1 cup water
3 or 4 trout
¼ cup butter
4 oz. instant rice

Soak pineapple in water to reconstitute. Place several pieces of pineapple in each trout and sauté in butter until barely done. Heat pineapple water to boiling and add to rice. Simmer five minutes. Remove from heat and let stand for five minutes until liquid is absorbed. Serves two.

## Trout Chowder

> 1 pkg. dried hash-brown potatoes
> 2 to 3 Tbsp. onion flakes
> 4 cups water
> 1 bacon bar
> 2 to 4 small trout, cleaned and cut into pieces

Reconstitute potatoes and onions in water until soft, then bring to a boil and add crumbled bacon bar. Cook mixture for 20 minutes. Add trout and cook five to 20 minutes more. Serves three or four.

## Trout And Noodles

> 3 or 4 sliced dried mushrooms
> 2 cups water
> 1 pkg. beef, pork, or chicken Ramen noodles
> 3 or 4 trout
> 1 zucchini, grated
> 2 Tbsp. butter
> 4 oz. grated cheddar cheese

Soak mushrooms in water. Add noodles to water with mushrooms. Boil briefly. Debone trout. Sauté zucchini and trout in butter. Serve noodles topped with zucchini, trout, and grated cheese. Serves two.

## Walnut-Oat Patties With Cashew Sauce

> 1 cup quick-cooking rolled oats
> 1 cup chopped walnuts
> ¼ cup soy flour
> 2 tsp. salt
> 1 cup seasoned whole wheat bread crumbs
> ½ tsp. each of basil, tarragon, and thyme
> 2 Tbsp. peanut or cashew butter (optional)

At home, mix dry ingredients. Season bread crumbs with combination of herbs. Store in plastic bag. In camp, add enough water and peanut butter to hold mixture together. Form into patties and sauté in oil or butter. Serve with cashew sauce below. Makes two eight-ounce patties.

## Cashew Sauce

> ½ cup cashew pieces
> 2 Tbsp. arrowroot or cornstarch
> ½ tsp. salt
> 2 Tbsp. onion powder
> 1 to 2 Tbsp. soy sauce
> 2 Tbsp. melted butter
> 2 cups water

At home, pulverize cashews in blender or with rolling pin. Mix with other ingredients except water, and store in plastic bag. In camp, add water to dry ingredients and butter mix to form a smooth paste. Simmer, stirring constantly to prevent lumps. When mixture has thickened to a medium sauce, serve over the walnut patties.

## White Mountain Stew

> 3½ cups water
> ¼ cup black-eyed peas
> ¾ cup dried vegetable mix
> ¾ cup couscous
> 1 Tbsp. butter

Add water to black-eyed peas and mixed vegetables. Bring to a boil. Cook 10 to 15 minutes until water is absorbed and ingredients are tender. Five minutes before cooking is finished, add couscous. Serve with butter.

## Wonton Soup

> 1 pkg. (1 oz.) dried shrimp
> 1 pkg. wonton soup mix with pork
> 1 pkg. freeze-dried peas
> 3 cups boiling water
> 2 tsp. soy sauce

Add shrimp and wonton soup mix to boiling water. Let simmer five minutes. Add peas, and simmer one minute longer. Top with soy sauce. Serves two.

## Desserts—Healthy Ways To Satisfy A Sweet Tooth

### *Bay Cinnamon Coffeecake*

1½ cups biscuit mix
½ cup whole wheat flour
½ cup packed brown sugar
¼ cup powdered milk
1 Tbsp. melted butter
dash of nutmeg
1½ Tbsp. cinnamon
1 Tbsp. sugar
¼ cup raisins
¼ cup nuts

Mix first six ingredients with just enough water to make a stiff dough. Shape into large patty. Sprinkle top with cinnamon, sugar, raisins, and nuts, and bake in a covered frying pan over coals until done.

### *Fruit Cobbler*

1 cup biscuit mix
2 Tbsp. powdered milk
¼ cup packed brown sugar
1 tsp. cinnamon
8 oz. chopped dried fruit
¼ cup honey
⅓ cup water
liquid butter or oil

At home, mix first four ingredients. In camp, put the fruit and honey into a pot, cover with water, and bring to a boil. Dump the dry mixture into another pot, and add water and a couple squirts of butter or oil. Mix well, then drop into the boiling fruit liquid. Cook 10 minutes uncovered, then 10 minutes covered. Serves two to four.

### Hobo Popcorn

> 4 squares heavy aluminum foil, each 12 by 12 inches
> 4 tsp. cooking oil
> 4 Tbsp. popcorn
> string
> butter to taste
> salt to taste

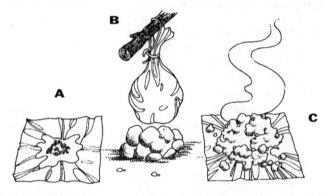

In the center of each foil square, place one teaspoon oil and one tablespoon popcorn (A). Bring corners of foil together to make pouches. Seal edges well, allowing room for popcorn to expand during cooking. Using string, tie each pouch to a long stick (B). Place pouch on hot coals and shake until popcorn is popped (C). Season as desired with butter and salt. Serves four.

### Mocha Pudding

> 1½ Tbsp. cornstarch
> 1 Tbsp. cocoa
> ½ tsp. instant coffee
> 3 Tbsp. sugar
> ⅓ cup powdered milk
> 1 Tbsp. butter flakes (optional)
> ¾ cup water

At home, mix dry ingredients, and store in plastic bag. In camp, empty contents of bag in pan and stir in water. Place over heat and continue stirring until pudding thickens. Serve warm. Makes one serving.

### *Norwegian Frukt Suppe (Fruit Soup)*

> 1 cup pitted prunes
> ½ cup raisins
> ½ cup dried apples or one diced apple
> 1 tsp. or 1 stick cinnamon
> ¼ cup tapioca
> berries

Boil prunes, raisins, apples, and cinnamon in water to cover. When almost tender, add tapioca and cook until it becomes transparent. Add berries, and serve hot or chilled.

### *Rice Pudding*

> handful of raisins
> 1 cup rice
> 1 tsp. salt
> 3 cups water
> 3 Tbsp. butter
> ½ cup powdered milk
> ½ cup packed brown sugar
> cinnamon to taste
> sprinkle of nutmeg

Add raisins and rice to boiling salted water and boil slowly until rice is done. Add butter, milk, and brown sugar. Stir, spice to taste, and simmer until thick.

### *Stuffed Apple*

> 1 apple
> 3 Tbsp. peanut butter or cream cheese
> 1 Tbsp. raisins or dash of sugar and cinnamon

Cut off the top quarter of the apple, remove the core, and stuff with peanut butter and raisins, or cream cheese mixed with a little sugar and cinnamon. Leave the bottom of the apple intact to contain the filling.

### Vanilla Ice Cream

> 1½ cups reconstituted milk, on the thick side
> 2 to 3 Tbsp. sugar
> pinch of salt
> 1 tsp. vanilla
> 1 tsp. instant coffee or cocoa, or banana or strawberry extract

Use fresh snow. When ingredients are mixed, add handfuls of fresh snow—the drier the better. Stir quickly. Instead of vanilla, flavor with instant coffee or cocoa, or banana or strawberry extract. Don't eat too much in cold weather.

# CREDITS

The information in this book is drawn from these and other articles in
BACKPACKER and WILDERNESS CAMPING magazines.

Buck Tilton, "Pooped In Paradise," BACKPACKER, October 1990, pp. 1-3

Cindy Ross, "Food For The Long Haul," BACKPACKER, May 1990, pp. 3-5

Marita Begley, "Food For Thought," BACKPACKER, September 1986, pp. 5-7

Terry Wood, "The Dry Fact," BACKPACKER, August 1991, pp. 7-9

Fred Bouwman, Mike Wyatt, Mark Jenkins, and Dave Getchell, "Just Say
'No' To Untreated Water," BACKPACKER, June 1992, pp. 9-14

Rob Lovitt, "The Big Chill," BACKPACKER, November 1988, pp. 15-19

Cindy Ross, "Cold Food," BACKPACKER, December 1989, pp. 19-20

Carolyn Gunn, "Withering Heights," BACKPACKER, August 1989, pp. 21-24

Steve Howe, "Desert Cool," BACKPACKER, June 1991, pp. 24-26

Bruce Franks, "Pouch Food," BACKPACKER, March 1989, pp. 27-29

Mark Sakry, "The Supermarket Trail," BACKPACKER, June 1989, pp. 33-39

Cindy Ross, "Bear Bagging," BACKPACKER, October 1990, pp. 39-43

Paul Cardwell Jr., "Camping Tips: Fireplaces," WILDERNESS CAMPING,
July/August 1972, pp. 50-54

Cindy Ross, "Rescuing Your Food," BACKPACKER, June 1992, pp. 55-58

Mike Wyatt, "A Garden In Your Pack," BACKPACKER, October 1990, pp. 58-61

Mark Sakry, "Foraging For Sea Food," BACKPACKER, May 1989, pp. 61-66

Mike Wyatt, "How To Eat Bugs," BACKPACKER, December 1991, pp. 66-68

# INDEX

Note: Page references in *italic* indicate illustrations.

**G**
Gas canisters, for pack stove, 45-47
Giardia cysts, 10, 14
Glasswort, 64
Gorp, 84
Goulash
    Meatless Goulash, 107
Granola
    Four-Grain Granola, 82-83
    Granola Bread, 85-86
    sugar free, 85
Grasshoppers, as food, 68
Gravy, 56-57
Grits
    Grits And Eggs, 76
    Grits au Gratin, 105-6

**H**
Ham
    Pea Soup With Ham, 110
High-altitude cooking, 47-50
High-altitude hiking, 21-22
Honey Bread, 87
Hottentot fig, 65
Hot weather, fluid needs in, 25-26
Hunter fire, 50, *51*
Hyperthermia, 25

**I**
Ice cream
    Vanilla Ice Cream, 118
Insects, as food, 66-68
Insulin, 3
Iodine, for water purification, 12
Irish moss, 63
Iron, 6, 18-19, 22

**J**
Jerky, 30-31, 87

**K**
Kelp, 66
Keyhole fire, 53, *53*
*Klebsiella pneumoniae*, 10

**L**
Legumes, protein-rich, 106-7
Lentils, 106
    Lentil And Rice Casserole, 106-7
    Lentil Stew, 107
    Meatless Goulash, 107
    Spicy Lentils, 108
Long-distance hikers, nutritional needs
    of, 3, 4

Lunch
    for cold-weather hiking, 19-20
    for high-altitude hiking, 24
    recipes, 19-20, 77-97

**M**
Matches, 38-39
Meat, 6, 7. *See also specific meats*
Milk
    Palatable Powdered Milk, 71
Molasses
    Molasses Hardtack, 88
    Molasses Nut Bars, 88-89
MSG, 28, 35
Muffins
    Carrot Bran Muffins, 80
    Fresno Bran Muffins, 83
Mung beans, 60
Mushrooms
    Curried Mushrooms, 103
    Mushroom Soy Stew, 109
Mustard seeds, 60

**N**
Noodles
    Chicken And Noodles, 32-33
    Chicken Sauce And Noodles, 101
    Trout And Noodles, 113
Norwalk virus, 10
Nutritional needs of hikers, 1-26
Nuts
    Bulghur With Fruit And Nuts, 98-99
    Cashew Rice Curry, 100
    Nut Cheese Loaf, 89-90
    Nut Soup, 109
    Nutty Wheat Balls, 90
    Spiced Pecans, 94
    Texas Spiced Pecans, 95
    Walnut-Oat Patties With Cashew
        Sauce, 113-14

**O**
Oats
    Backpacking Bars, 77-78
    Banana-Oat Energy Bars, 78
    Breakfast Booster, 72
    Camp Cereal, 73
    Canoe-Base Hudson Bay Bread, 79
    Familia, 74-75
    Hiker Cereal, 76
    Oatcakes, 90
    Peanut Polka Dotties, 91
    Walnut-Oat Patties With Cashew
        Sauce, 113-14